INDEX
FUNDS & ETFs

What they are
and how to make them
work for you

DAVID WOO SCHNEIDER

DAVID SCHNEIDER

Copyright © 2018 by David Schneider. All rights reserved.
Published by Writingale Publishing, LLC

No part of this book may be reproduced in any form or by any electronic or mechanical means, including information storage and retrieval systems, without written permission from the authors, except in the case of a reviewer, who may quote brief passages embodied in critical articles or in a review. Trademarked names appear throughout this book. Rather than use a trademark symbol with every occurrence of a trademarked name, names are used in an editorial fashion, with no intention of infringement of the respective owner's trademark.

Although the author and publisher have made every effort to ensure that the information in this book was correct at press time, the authors and publisher do not assume and hereby disclaim any liability to any party for any loss, damage, or disruption caused by errors or omissions, whether such errors or omissions result from negligence, accident, or any other cause. The information in this book is distributed on an "as is" basis, without warranty. Although every precaution has been taken in the preparation of this work, neither the authors nor the publisher shall have any liability to any person or entity with respect to any loss or damage caused or alleged to be caused directly or indirectly by the information contained in this book. The material contained herein is not investment advice. Individuals should carefully research their own investment decisions and seek the advice of a registered financial planner where appropriate.

Writingale Publishing also publishes its books in a variety of electronic formats. For more information about Writingale Publishing products, visit our Web site at www.thewritingale.com.

ISBN-13: 978-1545291856
ISBN-10: 1545291853

First Edition: April 2017

MEDEN AGAN – *'NOTHING IN EXCESS'*

CONTENTS

INDRODUCTION 1
PART ONE: A Little Something for Everyone 7
   CHAPTER 1 Index Funds: A Biography 9
   CHAPTER 2 Index funds, what are they good for? 35
   CHAPTER 3 Big fish in a little pond 45
PART TWO: The Index Fund Minefield 55
   CHAPTER 4 Problems of Theory 57
   CHAPTER 5 Problems of participation 77
   CHAPTER 6 Problems of narrative 89
PART THREE: Solutions 117
   CHAPTER 7 Salvaging indexing 119
AFTERWORD 141
GLOSSARY 148
ABOUT THE AUTHOR 151
NOTES 154

INTRODUCTION

As index funds, particularly equity index funds, were designed for, and are promoted to, retail investors, this book is for them.

Everything written herein is aimed firmly at the working man and woman – those who the investing business would dub "retail" investors. A defining quality of this segment is that they all tend to have to make plans for their retirement. If you've been burnt, in any way, by the two crashes since 2000, and are tired of advisors, "revolutionary" investment products and services that promise the world, but just end up providing meager returns or worse end in losses, this book is for you.

The purpose of this book is to help you understand what index funds and passive investing really are, and how these can be used in a manner that preserves your capital and increases it in an efficient manner. It is a guide on how to use your money for your own benefit, and not only that of the industry, which has unfortunately happened many times before in the history of Wall Street.

The Rise of Index Funds

Over the last five years, index funds and their ETFs (Exchange Traded Funds) have seen disproportionate growth, coinciding with the rise of computerized trading, mechanical and highly quantitative forms of investment management, and increased interest in the media. With its success, we can hear increasingly louder voices telling us that index investing (also known as "passive investing") is far superior to any active form of investing – such as actively picking stocks or mutual funds. And on the back of this, the entire industry has grown spectacularly. From its humble beginnings in 1976, index funds have grown into a $4 trillion Leviathan. Today, index funds make up over 30% of all mutual fund assets in the US, and they continue to grow. To be clear, when we talk about index funds and ETFs, we are talking about the same thing. ETFs on indices are index funds; it's just how they are bought and sold that distinguishes them foremost. Both their key characteristics and their particularities will be discussed in this book.

Proponents And Their Arguments

Index fund proponents include the crème de la crème of financial academia and the most respected professional money managers, such as Berkshire Hathaway's Warren Buffett, or Yale Endowment's Chief Investment Officer David Swensen. Add to this mix a growing number of nonfinancial celebrities, such as Tony Robbins, and the pro-index fund camp is formidable. Charles Ellis, famed investment consultant and author of "The Loser's Game," believes that active investment management is a "loser's game" and most of us shouldn't even try to beat market average returns, but instead should join the 'Index Revolution.' Index investing represents a superior investment strategy, and everyone should use index funds as the core of their investment portfolios." Burton G. Malkiel of Princeton University, one of the earliest and most avid proponents of index fund investing asserts: "Buying a low-cost index fund or exchange-traded fund (ETF) is the superior investment strategy." These proponents will back their recommendations up with a flood of data, like this snippet from consultancy DALBAR Inc.: "An investment of $100,000 made in 1984 grew to $296,556 over the 30-year period for an average equity fund investor, while the same amount invested in the S&P 500 grew to $ 2,358,275."[1]

The main argument of proponents of index funds is that investors can earn market returns at a much lower cost to themselves, and with full transparency. They argue that through plenty of diversification (owning as many as thousands of different stocks from different companies), you are protected from market variances. Investors can keep on contributing on a regular basis without actively having to research their investments and implying that any price will do, as long as the "long-term" is kept in mind, a key term you will hear several times over the course of this book. Index funds thus have been touted as not just for the middle class and masses of retail investors, but also large institutional investors, such as pension and endowment funds.

Another favorite prediction is that prices, and hence the index funds that they follow, will always rise. Many index fund proponents predict that stock markets will continue to rise to the tune of 8% to 9% per year just like clockwork – proponents that include Jack Bogle, founder of the Vanguard index fund – the first ever opened for retail clients.

Furthermore, proponents point out that index funds don't trade at all for capital gains as traditional mutual funds do, so they have significant tax advantages – capital gains tax only applies when clients sell their funds. And not just that – you can keep track of your investments from the comfort of your home! For example, if you buy an S&P 500 index fund, you only have to open the local newspaper to see how your fund is doing. It's a very transparent way to invest, and most buyers intuitively understand that they benefit from the success of those companies held in an equity index, and suffer from failure. Could it get any easier?

The Catch

However, not all is as rosy as people would make out. If you've been in the investment game for any length of time at all, you'll notice that very similar arguments are made for the all-time favorite investment – real estate. As an individual asset class, it too enjoys a lot of favorable tax treatment; furthermore, no one can deny that real estate is a tangible asset.

The parallels go further than that. Much like real estate before the crash of 2008, the current index fund system is what we call a "momentum play." The more people invest, the more other people invest, and the popularity of the product soars. Eventually, we get to the point where large masses of average retail investors jump on the bandwagon. More capital attracts more capital, which pushes prices higher and, for a while, predictions of never-ending growth seem true.

So how do we know this is what's happening with index funds? Well, let's look at the statistics. Though index funds have existed since 1976, their market share has always been below 10% for most of its 40-year history. Only since 2008 has this mark been significantly broken through, that now is projected to exceed 30% in 2017. Assets managed by index funds rose even more dramatically, from $11 million in assets by the end of 1976, to less than $900 billion in 2005, to over $4 trillion in 2016.[2]

The parallels between real estate and index funds are not absolute; index funds and their ETFs are just a form of mutual fund for various financial asset classes represented by an index. Because they don't do anything other than replicating an index, you can have index funds for any asset class imaginable including index funds on just the real estate sector. Nevertheless, we can't deny a pattern that looks only too familiar. In fact, you can go back much further to see the terrible effects of momentum plays – from the tulip mania in 17th century Holland, to the Dotcom bubble in 2000.

What Next?

This book is not a discussion of which asset class or investment is superior to others. But if you have been enticed by the index fund success story, and if you're thinking of investing in index funds, it's vital to know your basics in order not to repeat the same mistakes of the past. Rather than emulating generations of previous losers, learn from their mistakes.

First, we will learn what index fund, ETFs and their differences are, and explain why they are so popular by looking at the history of their three main characteristics – accessibility, flexibility and affordability. After that, we will examine the benefits and advantages of passive investing and why index funds and ETFs are being hailed by academia and professionals alike. Then we will examine the shortcomings and risks of investing in index funds, with a particular focus on the conventional approach to investing in index funds suggested by the proponents and the index fund industry itself. In the last section, I will offer an alternative approach on how to use index funds efficiently, and to your advantage.

Disclaimer

I am in no way a benefactor of the money management industry, nor am I promoting any particular fund, fund manager, fund company or financial advisory services. I am a self-published author and independent investor with over 20 years of experience in the field of investing and financial markets from both professional money management, as well as an individual investor's perspective. I have seen and experienced the inner workings of investment banks and institutional money management and I have experienced several financial crises with my own portfolio over the short course of my investment career. Hence, I am free to write with an objective view on index fund investing, their proponent's investment ideology and the organizational complex behind it.

If you want to learn more about investing, 80/20 investing in particular, feel free to visit my website www.8020investors.com and download one of the free resources that will help you improve your investment success.

DAVID SCHNEIDER

PART ONE

A Little Something for Everyone

DAVID SCHNEIDER

Chapter 1
Index Funds: A Biography

The mutual fund industry has been built, in a sense, on witchcraft.

– John C. Bogle

The disasters of 2001 and 2008 made investors wonder where all their monthly contributions went. Being burnt twice in the course of less than 10 years, most realized that they might always be on the losing end – with the mutual fund industry getting bigger and fatter, while they approached retirement in poverty.

However, with the lack of alternatives and their savings only yielding a pittance, the majority of existing retail investors felt they had no choice but to remain invested in stocks. With interest rates at historic lows, the only sensible solution seemed to be to give stock market investing yet another try. As a close friend recently explained, "One has to put one's money to work somewhere!" This time everything should be different – more transparent, easier to understand, and most importantly, cheap. The consensus is that nothing fits the bill like index mutual funds. It's no surprise that there is currently more than 30% of the $16 trillion mutual funds industry kept in these funds. The mutual funds industry itself is gigantic beyond any measure. It holds almost a quarter of all US household financial assets and 60% of all the money in individual retirement accounts – and the trend is upwards. So to begin, let's answer two crucial questions: What is a mutual fund? What is an index?

What Are Index Mutual Funds?

According to the Merriam-Webster definition, a mutual fund is "an open-end investment company that invests money of its shareholders in a usually diversified group of securities of other corporations." Professionals on Wall Street refer to them as "collective investment vehicles," as they collect money from more than one individual. Federal securities regulation dating back to 1940 refers to them as "open-end investment companies."[3]

You, as a client, buy a piece of this corporation – a piece called a fund share. These shares are issued on an ongoing basis and can be redeemed at the fund's current value, its Net Asset Value (NAV). NAV is a daily representation of all the assets possessed by the fund, minus all liabilities, divided by the number of shares outstanding. It's usually calculated once a day, often a couple of hours after the financial markets officially close. On the whole, it's not so different from buying shares in IBM or General Electric – transactions which also entitle their buyers to profit from their gains and give them voting rights. The difference is that the money paid for the shares is not there to finance supercomputers or electric power generators, but rather, to buy the securities in those companies that create these goods and services.

After you decide how many shares you want to buy, you transfer money to the fund and you are handed documents that testify to your partial ownership. In the meantime, the money you transfer to the fund flows into a bank account of a custodian bank. The bank pools and keeps the money and all portfolio purchases that belong to all shareholders. This is to legally separate the fund's assets from the advisor's assets. The custodian bank receives its sole instructions in regards to trading activities and money inflows and outflows from the fund's investment advisor.

The accounts themselves are administered by independent and reputable financial institutions, also known as fund administrators.

Their job is to make sure that all numbers add up and the fund "advisor" (i.e., manager) is not diverting money from the custodian accounts to their own pockets.

Investment "Advisors"

One strange characteristic of mutual funds is that they are made up of two legally separate entities – the fund (the pot of money itself) and the advisor (the management). Legally, the fund is a wholly-owned subsidiary of the advisor.

In a way, "financial advisor" is a misnomer, as the Securities and Exchange Commission (SEC) itself noted. As creators of the fund, the advisor manages and controls the fund, rather than merely "advising" it. All actions at the fund level are determined by these "investment advisors." The funds are managed, marketed and distributed by these advisory companies: Fidelity, Wellington, PIMCO, and all the other giants of money management.

Investment advisors need special licenses and must adhere to strict regulations to avoid past mistakes. A natural side effect is that the barrier to entry for setting up mutual funds has increased over the past decades. Moving forward, there is a trend towards consolidation in the mutual fund industry, and the concomitant growth in asset size will be one of the more important trends in managing money for others going forward.

Indices And Benchmarks

Richard Ferri, the author of *The Power of Passive Investing,* defines indices as follows:

> "An index is a generic term that describes a list of securities that are selected and weighted according to a set of rules provided by an index provider, and independent organization separate from index fund

management."[4]

So, how does this work? Let's imagine you wanted to create your own fantasy portfolio of all the famous brand names you like, such as Nike, Apple or McDonald's. You write them all down on a piece of paper and rank them by size, or by how much you like their logo, or by the results of personal surveys you did among friends and on social media. You compile this data, add the current market prices to each of these companies, and modify them by your chosen weightings. You might, for example, reduce McDonald's because they did very poorly in the last quarter, or boost Nike because you just bought a new pair and they're pretty good. Voilà, you have your own index!

Needless to say, it's not as simple as that. Not everyone can create an index that is widely followed and trusted. Even fewer could actually demand money for revealing their secret index mix. Only a handful of companies in the world can do this.

By far the most important company in this industry is S&P Dow Indices, a subsidiary of Standard & Poor's (one of the rating agencies that so lavishly gave triple-A ratings on mortgage-backed securities that evaporated into thin air during the subprime crisis). Next consider famous country-specific index providers, which are usually spun out of financial journals and newspapers, such as the Financial Times FTSE 100 Index in the UK (Financial Times Stock Exchange), or the Japanese Nikkei 225 (created by the leading financial daily paper *Nihon Keizai Shinbun*, or "Nikkei").

Then, there are benchmark indices created directly by the financial exchanges themselves. The most famous ones are the German DAX and the leading European indices grouped under the STOXX series (organized and managed by the Deutsche Börse AG). Some financial institutions have also created their own indices. The most famous of these is the MSCI index series (formerly known as Morgan Stanley Capital International) and the Lehman Bond Index series (now owned by British bank Barclays). MSCI Inc., in particular, prides itself on having more than "160,000 consistent and comparable indices, used by investors around the world to develop and benchmark their global equity portfolios."[5]

Financial market indices have broadened in terms of what actually counts as one over the years. All that a fund requires to qualify as an index fund is to have a mechanical set of rules for security selection, how they are weighted, and how they are priced. So anyone who has something to say about stocks and financial market instruments could create their own index.

Nevertheless, index fund purists insist that true index investing is all about benchmark market indices, which "represent an entire stock market and thus track the market's changes over time." Keep in mind that this definition applies not only to stock markets, but also to all other asset classes that can be represented by an index, and that is pretty much everything. Generally, broad market and market segment stock and bond indices are used for this purpose. In other words, they are used as a yardstick to measure active management performance; they're used in economic analyses to measure the level of market activity; they're used by academics to define market behavior; and they're used by investors to set asset allocation policy. But most importantly, benchmark indices are the basis for the largest and most famous index funds of the world.

Combining Mutual Funds And Indices

Index funds, in their purest form, are nothing more than mutual funds with a mandate to mirror the development of a chosen financial market index – nothing more, and nothing less. They have been a convenient tool for investors to participate in the price performance of an index. So, what exactly happens when you combine mutual funds with indices?

First, the mutual fund in question needs to get in touch with the index provider and ask for permission to mirror that index. Any mainstream mutual fund company that intends to create an index fund and mirror one of those reputable indices has to pay for that right. It's a licensing business. After all, it's all hard work, and if you created the index, you want to get paid for it, especially when others make money on your name. Sure, fund companies could create their own indices that resemble the leading market benchmarks, but they sure wouldn't sell as well as those of leading brand indices we can see in newspapers and on TV today.

Once all legal and financial matters are sorted out, the mutual fund receives the index "recipe." In this thick pamphlet, you will find all the index's rationales on how it has selected each constituent stock, and, more importantly, all the details how it calculates, weights and measures the different holdings within the index.

Now the real work starts. The index "advisor" (remember, these are the guys who actually run the show) instructs securities brokers and banks to invest in it in accordance with their interpretation of the index. Once all the money in the fund is deployed in accordance with the index recipe, all that is left to do is to monitor and administer the fund. Because mutual funds are designed to provide liquidity on a daily basis, and to continuously issue new shares for existing and new clients, there is always something to do. Clients leave and withdraw their money on a daily basis, while dutiful 401(k) savers provide inflow. From the advisor's perspective, the key task is to make sure *there is always enough money in their system to keep investing*.

Another source of work for the advisors is corporate events, such as dividend issues and splits and mergers of companies within an index. Also, the index regularly updates its recipe, kicking out companies and bringing in new ones. Remember, funds don't pay generous license fees on a subscription basis for nothing – there needs to be a semblance of added value by the index provider to justify continuous fees.

In a rare corporate visit to Vanguard in 2016, Bloomberg News had the chance to look behind the scenes of Vanguard Index Fund operations at their main office in Malvern, Pennsylvania, and to interview Gerry O'Reilly, manager of the $450 billion Vanguard Total Stock Market Index Fund (which matches the performance of its 3,600 stock benchmark index). What stands out is the efficiency of the 18 traders responsible for Vanguard's entire US portfolio and a senior manager most clients have never heard of. Yet, O'Reilly is responsible for $800 billion in assets. Star fund managers, those who are often quoted in the financial press and celebrated by loyal 'groupies, ' have no room in index fund operations.

Yet, whether you are an index fund proponent or hardened naysayer, no financial product exists in a theoretical vacuum. It is, therefore, vital to study the history of the structure, advantages and flaws of index fund investing and their providers. In this chapter, we will look at how index funds emerged out of a long history of scams, successes, failures, and legislative coups. For the purposes of this book, we will place a particular emphasis on the evolution of equity index funds and the accompanying theory of "passive" investing. In essence, there are three key qualities of index funds that are touted on – their accessibility, their flexibility, and their affordability. Looking through their history will help us understand how each of these qualities came to be associated with them.

The History of Index Funds

To trace the roots of mutual funds, we have to go back to the age of steam and sail, when Europe was scrambling to carve up Africa and the world witnessed the rise of the first great industrial barons of the late 19th century. By then, people had already begun to collect money from willing punters for the purpose of investing it in other people's enterprises. The original idea to pool money and diversify risk in different holdings and across countries was actually a Dutch one. A Dutch merchant, Adriaan van Ketwich, had the foresight to pool money from a number of subscribers to form an investment trust, the world's first mutual fund, in 1774. The first British investment trust was the Foreign & Colonial Investment Trust, founded in 1868, in order "to give the investor of moderate means the same advantages as the large capitalists in diminishing the risk of spreading the investment over a number of stocks."[6] The concept of money pools, known in those days as "investment trusts," had established itself as a mainstay by the 1880s in Britain. Individual investors would put their savings into these trusts, which in turn allowed them to invest in a diversified array of companies across the British Empire.

An excellent account of how these trusts functioned and thrived before 1929 is *The Great Crash*, 1929 by John Kenneth Galbraith. As he puts it: "The management of the trusts could be expected to have a far better knowledge of companies and prospects in Singapore, Madras, Cape Town and the Argentine [sic], places to which British funds regularly found their way, than the widow in Bristol or the doctor in Glasgow...The smaller risk and better information well justified the modest compensation of those who managed the enterprise." Hence, funds didn't just provide a mechanism through which to invest in big companies, they also embodied all the expertise required to do so efficiently.

The concept was soon exported to the United States, but the early trusts in America mostly maintained estates and trusts for their wealthy clients. Their primary goal was to conserve capital, rather than to multiply it – just as you would still expect from a family trust fund today. But what began as a noble idea to let professionals handle money, make use of public financial market investment opportunities, and use diversification to spread risk somehow got out of hand over the following decades. Eventually, it culminated in the epic Crash of 1929. No other book describes better and more vividly the lives of fortune seekers before 1929 than Edwin Lefèvre's *Reminiscences of a Stock Operator*. The biography of New England speculator Jesse Lauriston Livermore describes his progression from a day trader of his time in "New England bucket shops" (the early market-makers and manipulators) to the famed *market operator* at Wall Street, where he made – and lost – his fortune several times over.

Though Livermore had his personal office and secretary in downtown Manhattan, and mainly traded and lost his own money, some more savvy business operators understood early on the value of collecting and managing money for others. They found that those who just couldn't or weren't willing to directly participate were eager to entrust their money to people who seemed to know a lot more than they themselves did. They all wanted in on the American dream, and, more importantly, easy money.

Accessibility

Crucially, no one thought of this as being vital to their preparations for retirement. In fact, ideas of social security were still in their infancy; it was only in 1889 that the Germans, under Otto von Bismarck, introduced the first social insurance program. It was a revolutionary step mainly undertaken to keep the socialists in his country quiet, but also to give the working class a deserved financial future. At that time, no worker around the world would even dare think about playing the stock market in order to secure their future financial freedom. Before the Great Depression, the care of the poor was a responsibility assumed primarily by the private sector, generally through the extended family, friends and neighbors, and organized private charity. Retirement concerns were still managed conservatively and traditionally. Working, saving a portion or investing in some local enterprises, and spending the rest of your life in familiar environs with children and grandchildren (who were, in a way, investments and retirement insurance themselves) were the backbone of their social security.

This situation abruptly changed from 1928 onwards, when everyone, from the shoeshine boy to the corporate executive, had stock tips and read the *Wall Street Journal*. However, this was limited to a few living in the largest metropolitan cities on the East Coast. And those experts working on and around Wall Street were aware of whom they were dealing with. The familiar Wall Street term "sucker" comes to mind; it expresses the extreme contempt for those most gullible of victims. In the years leading up to the fateful events in 1929, the entire Wall Street elite behaved as if they were in some sort of financial Wild West. They developed schemes to extort money from their clients. Insider trading was rampant, and market manipulation and front-running were considered nothing out of the ordinary.

For example, market-moving news in Manhattan would take hours to reach the West Coast. It was entirely possible for people with solid routes of communication to hear news hours, or even days, before it became public. This time advantage gave the savvy a clear edge over less savvy players. And though they sold quickly before the terrible market news hit the ticker, making the downward movement even worse, many amateurs and dilettantes didn't even have a clue what was going on.

Into this world stepped the investment trust – institutions that presented themselves as capable of giving the big boys a run for their money. By establishing themselves in the market, creating their own routes of communication, and handling enormous sums of money, they were able to go toe-to-toe with the most powerful individual players in the market – the likes of the JP Morgans, the Vanderbilts and the Rockefellers. Funds such as State Street Corporation (established in 1792) and U.S. Trust Corporation (established in 1853) rapidly gained momentum and solid reputations. Assets managed by these trust companies ballooned.

Galbraith described this market frenzy in a chapter titled "In Goldman Sachs We Trust." When Goldman launched its own trust in December 1928, "$100 million of stock was issued, of which 90% was sold to the public. This was put in other stock selected in accordance with the superior insights of Goldman Sachs. In February, the Trading Corporation was merged with the Financial and Industrial Securities Corporation, another investment trust. Assets were now $235 million."[7]

Trusts were the upstarts of their time, and they were designed not for the bigwigs and robber barons of the time, but for the common man – or so it would seem. As a form of raising money, pooling and managing money, investment trusts had the leeway and freedoms that today's money manager could only dream of.

The trusts were able to leverage themselves without any restrictions or requirements of any permission from trust holders. These investment trusts looked a lot like modern day trading pools, with the difference that they could pile up debt to leverage any potential gain.

What began as a prudent system of capital management quickly degenerated into something not that far from the boiler rooms of the 1980s – groups of highly leveraged businesses desperately seeking any information they could get their hands on, and investing wildly, on margin, in everything in sight. In the end Galbraith said, "investment trusts were just another in a long line of clever Wall Street innovations designed to separate investors from their money."[8]

The number of trusts ballooned with what we would call today "product proliferation," and their quality declined inversely. An SEC report from 1934 identified that forty trusts opened in 1921 alone. At the beginning of 1927, the same report noted there were 160 such trusts, and another 140 were established during the year. During 1928, an estimated 186 investment trusts were established. By the first months of 1929, investment trusts were launched at the rate of approximately one each business day, and a total of 265 were brought to the market that fateful year.[9]

But what was going on deep inside all these trusts would shock any law-abiding fund manager and naive-thinking investor today. Galbraith tells the story of how Goldman Sachs Trading Corp applied increasing amounts of leverage via a weird sort of shell game in which one leveraged closed-end fund bought shares of another leveraged closed-end fund, which bought shares of yet another leveraged closed-end fund. "The idea," Galbraith tells us, "was to create a shell company or holding company that would sell debt and equity securities to the public and then invest that money – less management fees, of course – into the shares of other publicly traded companies."[10]

The gambling public had no idea how much leverage was used and what exactly these funds were invested in, since disclosure rules were extremely weak back then. The financial services industry showed itself utterly lacking in any sense of fiduciary duty or self-responsibility, and most people were none the wiser. If you've ever tried making sense of the financial news today, you'll get a feeling of how jargonistic and confusing it can be. Well, this is nothing new; in fact, it was probably worse in the 1920s.

The 1929 stock market crash is conventionally said to have occurred on Thursday, the 24th and Tuesday, the 29th of October – the two dates that have respectively been dubbed "Black Thursday" and "Black Tuesday." On September 3, 1929, the Dow Jones Industrial Average reached a record high of 381.2. At the end of the market day on Thursday, October 24, the market was at 299.5 — a 21% decline from the high. On this day, the market fell 33 points – a drop of 9% – on trading that was approximately three times the normal daily volume for the first nine months of the year. By all accounts, there was a selling panic. By November 13, 1929, the market had fallen to 199. By the time the crash ended in 1932, stocks had lost nearly 90% of their value. But that would be the initial stage of "an unprecedentedly large economic depression."[11] The Great Depression would continue for almost 10 more years, shaping the minds and memories of generations to come.

In the immediate weeks and months after Black Thursday, it wasn't only the massive price declines that kept America on edge, but the enormous scale of embezzlement that came to light. What Galbraith calls "psychic wealth" or simply "imaginative wealth" never existed . He described it like this:

> "...the person being robbed was unaware of their loss whilst the embezzler was materially improved. With the bursting of the bubble, accounts were now more closely scrutinized and reports of defaulting employees became a daily occurrence after the first week of the crash."[12]

The biggest losers in all this were individual investors who trusted in the capabilities of their managers and advisors. The real tragedy was that they lost most of their initial investments or, worse, had to pay outstanding liabilities, as they had made their purchases on borrowed money. The result of all this was a "deep freeze" that crushed the investment market until the 1950s. However, the precedent that these funds set – allowing common people to buy their way into the market with small deposits of capital, pooling these, and competing with the big boys – remained unchanged.

Flexibility

In the aftermath of 1929, Wall Street and the money management industry collapsed. Between the sudden loss of public trust and the weight of regulation, the entire sector entered what I like to call its first financial "Ice Age." This was a bear market so extreme and prolonged that it caused a paradigm shift among market participants until the 1950s. The general public came to openly despise anything that had to do with Wall Street, stock operators and their sales henchmen. During this time, and unlike today, any self-respecting, new graduate from the leading universities would avoid Wall Street at all costs.

It became obvious that reform and regulation were necessary, causing President Franklin D. Roosevelt to pass the Securities Acts of 1933 and 1934 and the Investment Company Act of 1940. His most potent regulation was the Glass-Steagall Act of 1933, which would separate commercial banking and investment banking for many decades to come.[13]

The financial industry would survive this financial Ice Age, licking its wounds and readying itself for a dramatic comeback. And when it returned, it did so with a vengeance, and with a whole new array of ideas, institutions, and investment vehicles to once again entice the people with money to hand their savings over to the siren call of big returns. In hindsight, the whole debacle of 1929 to the 1950s (and future dramas in the 1970s), though long and painful, would just be a speed bump for a concept that would grow to a multi-trillion dollar industry today. But in the immediate aftermath, what was needed was a new form of pooled investment vehicle, free and untouched, that kept all the same ideas of managing money as a business opportunity, but marketed differently. What emerged out of the ashes of the Depression was the modern *mutual fund*.

Mutual funds were a natural evolution in the world of money management. The main idea of a trust before 1929 was, according to Galbraith to create shell companies, or holding companies, that would sell debt and equity securities to the public and then invest that money. Mutual funds eagerly presented themselves as being different.

Pre-1929 trusts were based on the idea that only a limited number of shares were offered to the public, "After that, participation in the fund was available only by buying shares from existing shareholders in the open market."[14] Today, this is known as a closed-end fund. Unfortunately, this concept comes with limitations and some serious side effects. Because the numbers of shares were limited from the beginning, it made it more desirable for investors who wanted in, pushing the prices of the shares higher and higher, even if the underlying funds from the original subscription weren't properly invested in. In short, it encouraged speculation not only on the fund manager's level, but also on the level of shares; overly eager retail investors were willing to buy at any price just to get into a popular trust vehicle.

Mutual funds, on the other hand, were structured in a particular way that allowed them to issue new shares on a continuous basis, curbing any potential speculation in its own shares from the beginning. Retail investors were able to buy shares worth, let's say $100, and they would receive the same value of the investment fund's assets in return, measured as NAV. This concept is known as *open-end* funds. This afforded them another key characteristic of modern index funds – the *flexibility* to issue new shares as and when they choose, and, for those who own them, to sell them as and when they please.

Another important difference between the early trusts and the new mutual funds was that "in case of a mutual fund, the share owner, or beneficiary, had chosen the fund he wanted to invest in and had thereby granted the fund's managers the right to reinvest his money, for a fee…The managers of the fund are not trustees but investment advisors, and are therefore bound not by the laws governing trustees but rather by those governing investment advisors."[15] In the end, it was that new regulation, specifically regulating investment advisors, that would bring back the public's trust in money management and allow mutual funds to take center stage.

1924 was the birth year of the first two open-end mutual funds: Massachusetts Investors Trust and State Street Investing Company. A handful (19 in total by 1929)[16], survived the financial onslaught in the years between 1929 and 1934. Those that survived didn't use excessive financial leverage, as many trusts did, and their advisory firms didn't dump their toxic assets in them as many Wall Street firms (including Goldman Sachs) had before 1929.[17]

One of the few mutual fund pioneers was a small firm named the Wellington Management Company, founded by Walter L. Morgan in 1928. It was the investment advisory company to the Wellington Fund, one of the oldest surviving American mutual funds. It would also become the first workplace for a man who would decades later become the industry's fiercest "disruptor" and the most influential man in the history of index funds – *John C. Bogle*.

The rise of mutual funds was slow during the Great Depression, managing about $450 million in assets in the 1940s. By the end of the 1950s, the entire industry would record $2.5 billion in assets managed in only 1 million shareholder accounts. It was small in comparison with the $54 billion in life insurance reserves at that time.[18] But the Investment Company Act of 1940 helped restore public confidence in the financial system. It severely limited the actions of investment managers who managed money for the public, including the excessive use of leverage, shorting companies (speculating on falling prices), and the strict rule of diversification and avoidance of extreme concentration. All the old shenanigans were reserved for a close cousin of the mutual funds – the hedge funds, which continue to be major players in the field.

With a fresh set of new rules, the mutual fund business finally gathered steam. As people returned to stock market investing, Wall Street experienced a phenomenal comeback. The old marketing spiels were fired back up again, and the message was simple: through investments in mutual funds, the small investor could get expert advice, sufficient diversification and maximum action. "For the first time, ordinary investors with minimal capital could pool their resources in a professionally managed, diversified basket of investments, rather than going the more expensive route of buying individual stocks of varying risks. This was considered a giant step in the democratization of investments for the average person."[19]

Soon enough, the media began following the successes and failures of these new money experts who managed the dreams of those who believed in the marketing stories. This trend would eventually lead to yet another period of excess in the 1960s, known among financial historians as the "Go-Go Era."

No one reflects this better than Gerald Tsai. Born in Shanghai in 1928 to Chinese parents, he received a US college education and ended up with a degree from Boston University. He discovered a passion for stock markets, because, in his own words, "I felt that being a foreigner, I didn't have a competitive disadvantage there." If you pick stocks and they go up, it doesn't matter whether they were recommended by a Chinese, Indian or White Bostonian.[20] He learned the trade of managing modern mutual funds at a Boston investment firm, Fidelity Investments, which, under the leadership of legendary manager Edward C. Johnson II, would become one of the leading players in mutual fund management. Right from the start, Tsai operated in a way that was, at the time, considered outright gambling. He concentrated on a few stocks to their regulatory limit, purchasing giant positions throughout the trading day, only to sell most of them before the market closed, so as not to violate any investment advisory laws. Essentially, he sold a share for every one he bought – a technique unheard of at that time. His annual portfolio turnover exceeded 100% (similar funds in his category usually recorded about 30% portfolio turnovers). His behavior was often baffling. For example, after the Cuban missile crisis, he suddenly became very bullish on stocks. Within a period of six weeks, he put an enormous amount into stocks anticipating a quick stock market recovery. It paid off handsomely – the fund's asset value had risen by about 68% within three months.

But being a very ambitious man with an ego to match, he wanted his own firm to manage. Tsai left Fidelity and founded his own investment advisory firm in 1965. He named his new fund the Manhattan Fund because he had his new office on Fifth Avenue in Manhattan, far away from Fidelity in Boston. He was originally aiming to raise a conservative $25 million for his fund, but the fame he gained at Fidelity secured him an unimaginable $247 million. By mid-1968, the performance fund managed by Tsai had grown to over $500 million, with gross annual fees of over $2 million – a huge sum in those days. In the first years, his fund achieved an impressive performance of about 50%, on a turnover of 120%.[21]

Then, to everyone's astonishment, only a year later, he sold his management company to C.N.A. Financial Corporation, an insurance holding company, in exchange for an executive post with C.N.A and stock worth $30 million – again, a fortune in those days. Despite his departure from his own fund, in 1969 the world of money management still looked rosy. Mutual funds led by performance fund sales, held assets of some $50 billion, and were buying and selling stocks at a turnover rate of 50%, or half of their portfolio per year. Only in 1962 was that figure 20%.[22]

But in hindsight, Tsai's timing was nothing short of brilliant. In 1969, the market took its first noteworthy downturn in almost a decade; from the highs of 1,000 in late 1968, the Dow dropped to 800 by late spring of 1969. It would continue its decline to almost 700 a year later, which would mark a temporary low. To make matters worse, the high-flying performance funds of the mid-1960s lost their magic and looked very shaky. As it turned out, most of those funds were stuffed with very illiquid, small and microcaps of young and obscure tech start-ups that couldn't be sold as fast as the sell orders from fund clients came in. Also, investors, in general, were no longer as willing to hand over their money. Instead, they wanted out, and, unfortunately, all at the same time. It caused a stampede and marked the end of the Go-Go years. Gerald Tsai, who arguably started the wave of overly aggressive and speculative funds, was the only one who got away with all his chips.

But that's not the end of the story. During the Go-Go years, more conservative investors identified a group of stocks that could seemingly do no harm as compared to small tech start-ups. They were called the "Nifty Fifty." It was a group of fifty indestructible, large cap stocks on the New York Stock Exchange with stellar growth track records during the '50s and '60s. The instructions on how to use them were simple: buy 'em, keep 'em, and buy 'em again as money became available. Don't worry, second-guess, or interfere at all. Their growth itself will take care of fund performance. If this sounds familiar to you, it's because it is! The names within this group sounded like the All-Star Team of their time. It included technology leaders like Xerox, IBM, and Texas Instruments; pharmaceutical companies such as Merck and American Home Products; retail trendsetters like Kmart and J.C. Penney; and consumer products stars Avon, McDonald's, Kodak, and Polaroid. It also included the leading financial institutions. In other words, it included all that America stood for – economic prosperity, global dominance, and most importantly, "growth."

While the "Go-Go Years" finally came to an end between 1969 and 1971, the Nifty Fifty group of stocks would defy all common sense and changing market momentum. It pushed the Dow Jones up again to 1,000 in September 1972. In that year, money was still flowing into funds that actively promoted this indestructible group of stocks, mostly from disgruntled investors of performance funds who were looking for new places to park their money. But, at the beginning of 1973, something fundamentally changed. The Federal Reserve worried about accelerating inflation increasing interest rates. It caused a fundamental shift on how money managers saw the financial world, causing market interest rates to rise to new highs not seen for a very long time.[23]

Despite investors being advised to hold on and be patient, they began to flee in droves. As usually is the case in a market panic, the collapse of the Nifty Fifty cost the majority of retail investors dearly. Cautious as they were, they jumped late on the raging bull of the late '60s, and as the bull market continued, progressively bought more stocks at higher prices. When things dived, they held on the longest, lost the most capital, and emerged in the worst position, swearing never to return to stock market investing.

Whatever the suffering of all those losers was in the big game of money, at least the masses had a way of getting into the stock market with relative flexibility. But as those dramatic losses showed, not all was well with mutual funds. Academics in the field of economics and finance had been studying the subject of stock markets, management and their returns since the 1950s, and what they proposed would do honor to them and their field. Just as Isaac Newton applied mechanics into all facets of life in his time, financial economists applied math into everything they could lay their hands on, including financial markets and stock market performance. What they concluded was simple: masses of retail investors needed not only a flexible way to enter the stock market, but also an affordable vehicle for their money.

Affordability

Look back over the previous section and ask yourself: would you rather have invested in the Manhattan Fund without Gerald Tsai or held a spread of the Nifty Fifty? Keep in mind that after Tsai left, the Nifty Fifty actually outperformed all other managed funds for a while. So, what gives?

Academics in the 1960s noticed this, started analyzing mutual fund returns and their high-flying performance funds more closely, and began to wonder what, exactly, an active fund manager contributed to the performance of a fund. They were seeking a way to identify investment skill among managers so they might be able to copy those methods and use it to their own advantage – maybe even set up their own funds in the process. What they found surprised them. The data suggested that, after adjusting for risk (and luck couldn't be separated from skill), few active managers actually beat the markets. As a group, mutual fund managers had no special talents. The heavyweights in academics started to theorize that most investors would be better off just buying the market itself if they could, whereas another group of academics, mainly from the field of mathematics, kept rather quiet and set up their own hedge funds with some astonishing success. [24]

Nevertheless, their research started off the "passive" versus "active" debate in the 1960s. The traditional money management industry claimed that with their superior knowledge, training and resources, they were capable of adding value – in the form of better performance to the general market. But the academic data and research disagreed. Their argument was that the market was so efficient, and so many rational investors were looking at the same information, that it was impossible to outperform the market consistently. They dubbed this the "efficient market hypothesis" (EMH). If you put all professional and institutional money managers together, they already made up the large majority of the entire US stock market (with individual investors occupying the remainder).

Think about this: professional money managers represented most of the market. The market went up and down – it didn't just grow all the time. Hence, it was illogical that all of them were able to outperform each other. For the academics, the demise of the high-performance funds was proof that markets reverted to the mean, and periods of outperformance would lead to a period of underperformance, or even worse. What academics started to demand were so-called "market funds" represented by stock market indices; it was their logical conclusion.

Their research and rather brazen demands were not well

received by the money management industry. They rejected the academic findings as too theoretical, and nothing they could sell to a demanding public. Over and over, they would refer to the fact that there weren't any financial products that only mirror entire markets. And they were right; there weren't any index fund products in the offering until 1971. From then on, there were sporadic attempts by a few financial institutions to mirror leading benchmark indices, but they were poorly planned and executed. It needed a strong personality like John Clifton Bogle, a Princeton graduate – hardworking, ambitious, and ruthless – to overcome all major hurdles and launch such a revolutionary product.

In August 1976, the first publicly available index mutual fund was launched under the name "First Index Investment Trust" (later changed to Vanguard 500 Index Fund). That year, Bogle was the chairman of yet an unknown company, registered with the SEC under the name of The Vanguard Group of Investment Companies. This company originated from one of the oldest and most respected mutual fund companies – Wellington Management Company – where Bogle had been president and chairman only two years previously.

You might ask yourself: why such an abrupt change of position? At Wellington, he had always been a great operational manager and fervent promoter of Wellington Company, helping it survive the challenging period of post-war and the go-go years. He was what Edward Johnson, II, and Gerald Tsai represented at Fidelity – the necessary generation change. However, where Johnson would grow the Fidelity brand and finally pass on the reign to his son, who would later pass it on to his daughter, Bogle wasn't destined for the same smooth path. In some respect, it was his own fault. In the excellent biography by Lewis Braham, *The House That Bogle Built*, you can read up on a fascinating success story that, to a very large extent, reads more like a corporate thriller than a story about a man on a holy mission.

Vanguard originated out of a corporate power struggle at the top of Wellington Management that Bogle lost. It left him only the two options: to either leave Wellington completely or take over the administrative function of Wellington Funds in a separate legal entity. He opted for the latter, but with some aces up his sleeve.

Wellington's board didn't think much of Bogle's choice to become an administrator of the assets they controlled. He wouldn't have real executive power in making investment decisions, managing any money, or even raising funds. Wellington thought of Bogle's new position as a sort of consolation prize to soothe his personal pride. However, they underestimated Bogle's resolve. The new administrative entity, launched in May 1975, was called Vanguard Group (The Vanguard Group of Investment Companies).

It soon became apparent that he didn't see himself as simple administrator. Rather, he aimed to influence Wellington Management through the new power he gained at the fund company level – Vanguard Group. Strangely enough, the fund's board, which was distinctly different from the board of the investment advisor, had more power than Wellington had anticipated. This left Bogle with plenty of room to make life at Wellington more than complicated. However, one problem remained for Bogle and his newly formed entity. How could Bogle take over the money management function as well without violating his agreement with Wellington? How could he get more and more control of all the fund's investment management functions while slowly detaching himself from Wellington? It dawned on him that creating the first index fund was the perfect solution to circumvent (and not violate) his agreement to not manage any money – as technically no active advisory mandate was necessary for creating an index fund. After all, all he had to do was to copy a market index.

The plans for launching took shape in 1975, with Wellington strongly opposing it – but they had no say in it, as Vanguard technically wouldn't violate any of its agreement and Bogle controlled the fund's board. Finally, the Vanguard Group would launch the first publicly available index fund in August 1976. While being continuously sabotaged by Wellington in its sales and promotion efforts, it had difficulty warming up potential investors. The initial offering attracted only $11 million, far below the $150 million Bogle had targeted. Besides being in the second ice age, the general public just wasn't ready for this type of product yet. They still believed in the credo of beating the market indices as the ultimate goal of any self-respecting money manager. To top it all off, his colleagues from the traditional mutual fund management companies, including Wellington, ridiculed his foray into passive investing, calling it "unpatriotic," "Bogle's Folly," or accusing the rationale behind it of aiming to be "average" – a very un-American ideology, indeed. By the end of 1976, the Vanguard fund had grown to only $14 million.

Entering the roaring '80s, Vanguard would collect more and more assets through more and more fund launches. By the beginning of the 1980s, it had already collected $2.4 billion. By 1999, the year Bogle left as Chairman of Vanguard, the figure would be $540 billion. At the beginning of 2017, that number was about $4 trillion.[25] And all through these years, Vanguard was able to reduce its fees. By 2000, Vanguard was by far the lowest-cost provider, having slashed its expense ratio to 0.27% for its flagship funds, while the average fund charged 1.21%. Today, it charges only 3 to 4 basis points for some of its flagship funds to institutional clients.

The Vanguard 500 Index Fund (AUM)
From $11 million to $203 billion in 40 years

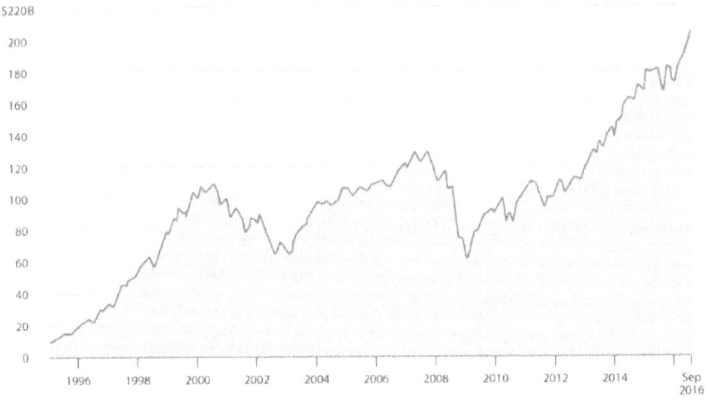

Source: Bloomberg

Vanguard's cost advantage was a direct result of its mission to become the low-cost provider by passing on any savings to clients. It achieved this through operational efficiency and the fact of just mirroring an index without engaging in elaborate research or forecasting. In addition to not having to pay for armies of expensive fund managers, research analysts and outside research resources, it has always had much lower marketing and advertising expenditures. With its growing asset size, Vanguard profited from an economies of scale effect, which allowed it to negotiate fees paid to external third-parties, such as brokers and banks. Over the years, through constant investment in technology, Vanguard was able to further improve operational efficiency. Technology enabled Vanguard to automate the entire investment and trading process, along with the administrative processes. With this obvious cost advantage came the "word of mouth" effect, as more and more people realized they were being charged high fees for subpar or even lousy returns. This, in turn, enabled Vanguard to raise more assets and lower cost even more.

It took some time until the industry caught up and understood the real threat that index funds posed to their existing business model. The large majority of professional money managers simply did not recognize the *disruptive potential* that the concept of indexing contained. Vanguard is, and remains, "the Walmart of money management," and in their hands the index fund as we know it was born – affordable, accessible, flexible, and dominating the industry. Buying shares of mutual funds remains very affordable. Anyone with a bit of money saved up can buy shares in mutual funds. The Vanguard Total Stock Market fund, for example, charges $50 for a single share, with an initial minimum investment of $10,000.

Index Funds And Their Indices

The origins of indices are not so different from the process described above. In 1884, Charles Henry Dow, editor of the *Customer's Afternoon Letter* (forerunner of *The Wall Street Journal*), wanted to give his readers an impression of the daily stock market situation. At first, he and his business associate Edward Jones, a trained statistician, created a group of 11 transportation stocks (train stocks being the big money-spinners of the late 19th century). His pioneering transportation average began in 1884. In 1896, he expanded this idea and created the Dow Jones Industrial Average (DJIA), which included 30 companies from the entire spectrum of the industrial complex of American business. Even today, the DJIA is still the most widely quoted stock indicator in the media. However, the Dow Jones had its flaws, and couldn't be used as the preferred indicator of US stock markets.

First, it only contains 30 companies, and it only included companies that its founders and today's successor considered "industrial stocks." A company such as Google (Alphabet Inc.) is not included in the Dow, even though it is one of the top three largest companies in the world, as measured by market capitalization. A more serious flaw for index aficionados is the fact that it is a simple price index, where all companies are equally weighted and only distinguished by their individual stock price quotation. A company like American Express would have the same impact as Apple has, even though American Express is much smaller in size as measured by assets and market capitalization (AMEX market cap as of December 2016 was $68 billion vs. $617 billion for Apple). In short, the DJIA is a simple price indicator and not an indicator of the overall value of a company.

These two major flaws were addressed in 1923 by the Standard Securities Corporation (now Standard & Poor's). S&P constructed the first capitalization-weighted index that took the market value of each of its constituents into consideration. Initially, there were only 90 securities in the index, but it would expand its holdings until it reached 500 securities in 1957. The new S&P 500 soon became a widely regarded benchmark for US equities markets, and the one most often used among industry professionals to this day.

Not surprisingly, the S&P 500 was chosen as the basis for the first index fund by Vanguard in August 1976. Starting in the 1970s, more companies entered the indexing business by collecting and tabulating market returns from around the globe and forming benchmarks. These firms included Frank Russell Company, Wilshire Associates, and Morgan Stanley Capital International (MSCI), to name a few. Most indices were created between 1970 and 2000 to give active managers a reference point to compare themselves against; by 2015, more than 9,000 funds were active in the US alone.[26]

Chapter 2
INDEX FUNDS, WHAT ARE THEY GOOD FOR?

> ...*some large foundations set up an in-house portfolio that tracks the S&P 500 Index—if only for the purpose of setting up a naïve model against which their in-house gunslingers can measure their prowess.*
> – Paul Anthony Samuelson

Now that we have a good understanding of the origins and functions of index funds, let's have a closer look at why you may want to consider investing in them. In this chapter, we'll look at some of the pros of index funds — information you need to have a good understanding of without the added spin by investment professionals.

Low Costs And Fees

When investing in an index, you don't have to pick stocks, select and research individual companies, consider which sector you should focus on, or which businesses in each sector should be watched most closely. All you need to do is buy a basket of stocks that has already been chosen by an index provider – usually by machine. All the work is effectively done by them, which means you don't have to pay for expertise or research. According to Jason

Zweig, personal finance columnist for The Wall Street Journal, "The machines that run index funds slash the costs of investing by 90% or more by skipping most of the research and trading."[27]

Thanks to enormous developments in computing power and sophistication of trading software, we have seen a revolution in how the world trades on financial markets. Vanguard, BlackRock and State Street have been quietly working on their own "autonomous economy" revolution. Where in active management, there are hordes of analysts, portfolio managers, and support staff with an average salary north of $100,000, less than a tenth of this human workforce is necessary at a well-equipped index fund operation. That's a lot of potential cost savings, and those savings give index funds a very decisive advantage when it comes to tracking past and future performance.[28]

Index Funds are also more tax efficient than mutual funds. All mutual funds offer tax benefits when offered through retirement plans such as a 401(k) plan, which calculates their contributions before tax deductions. But index funds add another layer of tax advantages because they trade much less frequently than actively managed funds, reducing the amount of tax they have to pay on capital gains . Moreover, index funds never pay out profits that they accumulate from the stocks they own in the form of dividends; the extra money is simply kept and reinvested. For example, if they own ten shares of company X, and make a 10% dividend, rather than paying it out to investors, they'll simply increase it by another share – ending up with 11. Hence, dividends become free money for the fund manager to play with – and, ultimately, the shareholders to benefit from.

Trumping Market Performance

Index returns are calculated by the income all companies generate in the form of dividend payments plus any capital gains measured from the beginning of a calendar year to the end of a calendar year. The leading index funds mirroring the S&P 500 generate returns that represent most of the US stock market's total returns. Hence, investors receive US market returns; that is, they benefit from the performance of the market as a whole.

However, it's not just that index funds are so fascinating for academics and fans; it's their performance relative to all actively managed mutual funds and the whole industry of money management. All reputable statistics indicate that index funds outperform around 85% or more of other mutual fund managers with similar investment objectives. According to Tony Robbins, "An incredible 96% of actively managed mutual funds fail to beat the market over any sustained period!"[29]

Based on some reports, 98.9% of US equity funds underperformed over the past ten years, as did 97% of emerging market funds and 97.8% of global equity funds.

That means index fund performance beats the vast majority of all professional US fund managers every year. Nearly all of the managers who beat the indices in one year almost certainly will not do it in the following years. Among academics, this phenomenon is called *mean-reversion*, a law that observes that outlier prices and returns eventually move back toward the mean or average. In other words, statistically, if an active investment manager beats the market one year, he is more likely to underperform by the same amount the next.[30]

The situation isn't much better over the pond in Europe. Four out of five active equity funds failed to beat their benchmark over the past five years, a figure rising to 86% over the last ten years, according to S&P's analysis of the performance of 25,000 active funds. According to the Financial Times, "Almost every actively managed equity fund in Europe investing in global and emerging markets has failed to beat its benchmark over the past decade, raising more questions about the value stock picking managers add to the whole investment process." In Switzerland alone, 95% and 88%, respectively, of those on offer in Denmark also underperformed. Daniel Ung, director of research at S&P Dow Jones Indices, said: "We are not saying active management is dead, but active managers need to justify what they are doing."[31]

The explanation for the stunning success of index funds is simple. Research shows that the root cause of index funds outperforming all experts is the savings they make from lean operational management. All the cost savings in workforce, expensive research, and other hidden fees give index funds a substantial head start when it comes to making money for clients. Where an active fund manager has to still make up 1% to 2% in fees and sales commission (not an easy feat in markets swamped with cheap liquidity and interest rates at close to zero, or even negative), index funds generate performance after covering 4 to 20 basis points. Remember that Vanguard charges its institutional clients just three to four basis points for its premier Admiral class of funds; retail clients in most 401(k)s are not charged much more.

Having worked at a traditional institutional money management company, I have seen internal work processes and policies, flaws and politics. I have seen top management panic whenever markets behaved unexpectedly or irrationally, as well as major political rivalries between asset manager teams, incompetent project managers and greedy IT consultants that made IT infrastructure investments a nightmare. Moreover, don't forget the elaborate marketing and sales operations whose job it is to suck money like a vacuum from targeted clients.

None of this should surprise you, especially when you're managing several billions of dollars across several countries. Any operation that size has its structural challenges. Fund managers have to adjust their portfolios whenever big economic news breaks. Central bankers sneezing or giving press conferences, politicians discussing fiscal policies or interns playing with cigars in the Oval Office – all this changes how fund managers and their analysts see future capital flows within each industry, and necessitates investment and trading decisions. Daily meetings with IR (Investor Relations) departments of large corporations and sales people from various brokers are the norm. (I particularly liked the German pastry we served at these meetings. Brokers never ate them as they were busy pitching their ideas. Our fund managers, listening with one ear, seemed to be more focused on gobbling them up. I, as a trainee, got the scraps after each meeting. Here's a piece of free advice: if you want to find out who the real power is in a company, look for the dude who gets to eat first and most.)

The bottom line is proponents of passive investing make a good point about their operational advantages over actively managed funds. Moreover, cost savings is the all-dominant factor. Just imagine how many cookies and pastry we had consumed at that time; index fund operations have none of that.

Avoiding Dilemmas

Constantly picking the right stocks or industry sector is certainly a *loser's game*. Picking the wrong stock within a sector has serious repercussions. Just imagine you underweighted Apple because the fund manager didn't believe in the new iPhone 7. But then, surprise! Apple shoots up. Suddenly your fund is underperforming for the next month while your General Motors stocks are as boring as before. You, sir, are in trouble.

It is even worse if you overweight the wrong industry. Imagine you underweight technology stocks during the biggest tech bubble the world has ever seen, and invest in shipping and retail stocks instead. In 1999, you would have been called the greatest idiot in the industry. Under pressure from senior management, you finally overweight the tech sector, gobbling up all those high-tech flyers, such as Cisco Systems and Amazon, only to see the dot-com bubble pop a couple of months later. Now you are called an idiot for not anticipating the end of the tech bubble. In a world where everything is measured on a monthly basis or even shorter time frames, that is a serious psychological burden for all involved in the money management industry.

Hence, most money managers tend to go with the conventional investment approach, because no one wants to be accused of going against the tide and lose his or her job for gutsy calls – even if he or she suspects that the conventional wisdom is wrong. In any case, if the markets go up, they're showered with praise. If markets go down, fund managers can blame it on the markets. So, it is no wonder most actively managed mutual funds do so with the same benchmarks, and tend to fly very close to the benchmarks they are supposed to beat.

Index funds are not concerned with these matters. Their job is only to track their selected index as closely as possible, to find ways to save operational costs or find additional sources of fund income. Equally, for retail clients it is much easier to focus on just market performance rather than worry too much whether they have chosen the right fund with the right fund manager who has the right investment strategy and who selects the right industry and the right stocks within that particular industry. Just sit back and watch the money roll in – until it doesn't anymore.

Transparency

Another advantage of index funds is their transparency. We have a wealth of data about their underlying indices. We can monitor and follow the leading benchmark indices in any reputable newspaper. The selection and composition of the index and the actual execution of investments are strictly separated, leaving nothing to willful manipulation – unlike the chicanery of some active managers who have tried to manipulate their NAVs and cheat their investors. Their purchase and administration are child's play. If you want to buy them, fill out an online form, upload some ID documents, enter your Social Security number, and transfer your money through your local bank. If you want to buy more, just fill out some additional forms and give permission to your mutual fund provider to withdraw money from your bank account automatically – the good old standing order. If you want out, just follow a similar procedure and wait until the money hits your accounts. If you want to know how your fund fares, follow the respective index in the financial news section of your local newspaper. If you want to know what is really in your fund, contact or visit the index provider and read up on their theoretical models and constituency selections.

Easy Purchasing

The most common way to acquire index funds is directly through fund management firms and their distribution channels. Let's assume you decided to invest $50,000 that you just saved up, and you are committed to contributing further on a monthly basis. Savvy as you are, you go to the market leader Vanguard and visit their website. As noted above, the buying process is very easy. You can purchase them at any time of the day, but the price for which you buy them is fixed only once a day, usually with some delay after market close.

For equity index funds offered by Vanguard, you can conveniently open an account with a blink of an eye; you can shuffle over your money to them through a domestic fund transfer. In fact, these days you can watch videos on YouTube that demonstrate how to buy index funds online and guide you through the process with live commentary and screenshots. It can't get easier than that. You transfer your money online from a local US bank address, and in return, you get a confirmation via mail saying you are now the lucky owner of Vanguard mutual fund shares. When you log in online, you see the same.

The other convenient way to participate in the index fund game is through so-called Exchange-Traded Funds (ETFs). The first exchange-traded fund – Standard and Poor's Depositary Receipts (SPDRs, popularly known as "Spider") – was created in 1993 by Nathan Most. The idea is simple. Rather than buying mutual funds from third-parties or directly from the issuing mutual fund provider, clients can buy mutual funds through stock exchanges. All the advantages of stock exchanges come to play, such as price transparency and guaranteed liquidity and settlement by a neutral third-party (the exchanges themselves). This way, mutual funds are able to reach more clients; exchanges get to make more product offerings and fee income; and brokers execute clients' orders and make a commission. Lastly, clients could trade mutual funds any time of the trading day.

The most important feature of ETFs is that they are open-end funds and continuously issue new classes of shares. This distinguishes them from their predecessors, the closed-end trust funds in the 1920s, which had a pre-set number of shares issued from the day they launched. By continuously issuing and redeeming new shares, ETFs can avoid price distortions due to demand and supply imbalances. In other words, ETFs can always trade closely to the listed prices of their underlying indices.

What was really revolutionary was not their complex legal structure and issuing procedure, but the fact that they were like any securities traded on exchanges. We can buy and sell ETFs all day long (as long as exchanges are open for trading). If you wanted in after lunch but out before dinner, no problem. If you changed your mind on the way home, just use your trading app and get back into your favorite ETFs just before markets close – all with a click of a button and minimal trading fees. A valid question would be: What does this have to do with long-term investing?

With traditional mutual funds, it's different. We can buy them directly from the provider without the need for an exchange, but we can trade them only once a day after markets close. In effect, any mutual fund that exists as an open-end index fund can be converted into an ETF. The advantages for retail investors is that they have a convenient way to enter the game with ETFs, which offer full access throughout the trading day, real-time prices, and a wide variety of fund styles and providers without having to open separate accounts with each fund provider. You can buy any listed ETF through your online broker at any time during trading hours. You can't do that with traditional mutual funds sales channels. It's not surprising, then, that ETFs have grown to be a huge part of the multi-trillion index fund asset base. In 2006, ETFs already made up a 41% share of all index fund assets, up from just 3% in their first year in 1993.[32] Today, that figure is even higher.

ETFs have been extremely successful new investment instruments, having grown over the past twenty years from nothing to more than $2 trillion. Much of this explosive growth has come from sophisticated institutional investors, such as hedge funds, rather than from individual investors. By 2014, an estimated 5.2 million, or 4%, of US households held ETFs.[33] The asset size of the US ETF business was estimated at $2.6 trillion by the end of 2016, which constitutes more than 13% of total net assets managed by mutual funds. There are estimates that there are about 4,396 ETFs globally, with about 1,400 domiciled in the US. That number is growing with more and more retail investors jumping on board.[34]

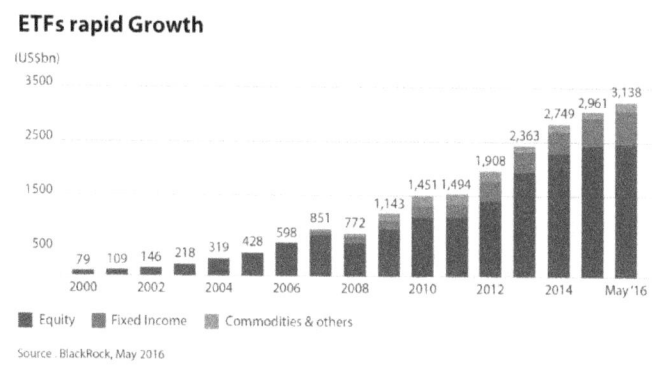

The three largest ETF providers, BlackRock, Vanguard and State Street, hold $2.13 trillion in assets under management (AUM) among themselves. The top three largest single ETFs are also provided by the same three companies – the iconic SPDR S&P 500 (Spider) with $212 billion AUM, an official expense ratio of 0.09% and provided by State Street leads the way, followed by BlackRock's iShares Core S&P 500 ETF and Vanguard's Total

Stock Market ETF.[35] It's clear that we will see much more from ETFs in coming years because they can be attractive for everyone involved, including their buyers. Unfortunately, as we shall see in Part Two, it's for the wrong reasons.

Chapter 3
BIG FISH IN A LITTLE POND

There's no such thing as a free lunch.
— Milton Friedman

The mutual fund industry as a whole has grown in asset size, even though active managers lost market share. Index funds with their ETFs have grown dramatically, and there are no signs of stopping this trend going into 2018.

People buying index funds tend to focus on the benefits for themselves, which is, of course, only natural. However, it is crucial to understand the picture from the perspective of other players in the biosphere called indexing. Index funds offer diverse advantages to everyone involved, including the index provider, the index fund providers; all the auxiliary services such as brokers, fund administration, financial advisors, lawyers or auditors; and all the companies index funds invest in. The money put into mutual funds and ETFs powers entire industries, creating jobs and lively capital markets. It even gives government institutions a convenient tool to put their own stamp on financial markets, and that indirectly profits index fund holders. It is rumored that Japan's central bank, the Bank of Japan (BOJ), is the largest single shareholder of Japanese stocks, thanks to their massive purchases of index ETFs on the open markets. This, in turn, helped prop up market prices.

What follows is a quick overview of the benefits for those on the supply side of index funds – the people you will be doing business with.

Index Creators

No one has profited more from the boom of index funds than the index originators themselves. It's one of the best business models on the planet. It's stable fee income for a product that does not require massive capital investments or any physical maintenance, inventory concerns or even regulation. It's an oligopolistic business model with a tendency to create monopolies in separate countries – similar to financial exchanges themselves. And since modern capitalism has a fetish for gigantism under cover of cost efficiency and growth, we now have a handful of index providers that dominate the global financial market. In 2015, there were 10,000 funds in the US alone, and they all use a benchmark or more for each of their funds – fee income for index providers – again, big and very easy profits. Just analyzing the business model of S&P Dow Jones Indices and MSCI would open the eyes of many index fund investors and mutual fund investors alike.

Here is a quick overview of MSCI key financial figures, by far the smaller player compared to S&P Dow Jones Indices. MSCI is itself is a publicly listed company and part of the S&P MidCap 400 Index. According to SEC filings, it boasts more than $1 billion in operating revenues for the year ending December 2015, operating income of over $400 million and net income of $220 million – not so bad for a business that creates fictitious pools of securities in all imaginable sizes and forms. Remember, MSCI alone currently offers more than 160,000 indices. Charles Dow, back in 1896, could not have imagined the industry he would create, all with a few yellow legal pads and a couple of pencils.

The Big Three

As a retail investor interested in conventional benchmark index funds, you could be focusing just on three giant fund providers: Vanguard, State Street and BlackRock. Together, they command more than $12 trillion in assets. For comparison, the entire US national debt is about $20 trillion, and its entire social security liability is about $15.6 trillion.[36]

Vanguard

Vanguard had the "first mover" advantage of being the first index fund provider. It has successfully catered to the masses since 1976. Today, it employs 15,000 people in 16 locations worldwide and commands a financial empire of over $4 trillion.

BlackRock

Founded in 1988, BlackRock brought itself into this position by gobbling up one index provider after another as part of a well-thought-out business plan to become the largest asset manager in the world. They acquired indexing teams that were part of the index game since back in 1971. Their most decisive purchase was Barclays Global Investors, provider of the famous iShares series of exchange-traded funds, in September 2009. This deal alone made BlackRock a force in the growing ETF market. However, it came with a price tag of $13.5 billion for something that is technically an empty shell with some computer servers and computer code. So to make a deal of the size of almost $14 billion work, BlackRock must have thought of it as a very lucrative business opportunity indeed, considering that they charge about ten basis points (0.1%), on average, for the money they command for their ETF division.

State Street

State Street has been part of the mutual fund success story from the very beginning. In fact, the State Street Investment Corporation, formed on July 29, 1924, was one of the three first mutual funds in the United States; the head of State Street Investment Corporation was Paul Codman Cabot, of the Codmans and Cabots, early Boston families that would later dominate money management with a distinct Boston culture.[37]

They would also make their mark on the index fund world. State Street was one of the few traditional money managers that understood the potential of index funds for amassing large amounts of money from clients. In 1993, State Street, in cooperation with the American Stock Exchange, launched the Standard & Poor's Depositary Receipts (NYSE Arca: SPY; now the "SPDR S&P 500"), the first ETF available through brokers. The "SPDR S&P 500" is still the largest and most widely traded ETF in the world.

Companies In The Index

Some of the biggest beneficiaries of the index fund boom are the companies that are inside an index themselves. Those outside an index have a miserable time struggling with reputation, liquidity, money and all sorts of other psychological side effects of not being included in an exclusive club. However, when you are in, boy, is it great!

Think about it for a moment: who would you rather want to have as a business partner and shareholder? A person who continuously meddles in your daily affairs and asks tedious questions, or a person who sits quietly in a corner and smiles at you whenever he or she visits you, which is usually once or twice a year. However, as it so happens, they also shovel money into your stocks on a daily basis without asking any questions of real importance.

Recently, I had a conversation with a couple of IR managers at some very large Japanese corporations. They confirmed that index funds are the ideal shareholders and cause very little trouble or concerns for their departments. They confessed that they very much looked forward to meeting with index fund representatives. Much more so than meeting with those dreadful hedge fund types who ask complicated questions and add no value to the relationship. They tend to sell after a few weeks or months, and at times, can get very nasty when they get impatient. The real winners of the index fund boom are giant public companies, as long as they remain in the "circle of trust" and a member of such an exclusive club.

Financial Advisors

The challenges of an optimal asset allocation reveal an old problem that we have as retail investors – it's easy to get lost in a jungle of jargon, theories, and product offerings. In that jungle of index fund product variations, it takes some serious guidance and hard work to cut through the many strategy alternatives and myriads of combinations of index fund portfolios. Aware of all these complexities and as average mortals with many things on our minds, wouldn't it be better for us to get professional advice?

An advisor's job is important, as they design tailor-made investment policies, oversee their implementation, and control and maintain such policies. Financial advisors and planners who have been specializing in index funds have just been replacing actively managed funds with index funds. Some proponents of index advisory suggest that their real role is being a shrink for its many insecure clients. Added value creation through enhanced monetary performance is difficult to prove and, in Bogle's own words, "Relying on even the best-intentioned financial advice seems to work only spasmodically,"[38] but advisors should always be there to soothe the weakened mind of each their clients in times of exuberance, and more importantly, in times of financial distress.

As we all know, financial advisors, and particularly index fund experts, don't come free. They are in high demand and require appropriate compensation for spending countless hours keeping up with existing and new product developments in the index fund realm. Hence, despite "passive" investment being pitched as an alternative to "active" investment by professional managers, in the end, a professional manager is precisely what you will need in the world of index funds.

Traders and Speculators

Index funds and their loyal investors are also providers of precious liquidity and trading opportunities for those with very different investment and trading philosophies.

All major participants in financial markets live in a symbiotic relationship. First off, there are the intermediaries. All these brokers and securities companies actually make it possible for mutual funds and individual investors to buy all those stocks within an index and, nowadays, more and more ETFs that are traded through brokers. Each trade that index funds do first profits their intermediaries. As minuscule trading commissions are in the age of electronic trading, the sheer size of the index fund markets is sufficient for intermediaries to earn a decent living just by greasing the wheels of trading.

Then there are those who are actually selling stocks to index funds – the sellers. They are those on the other side of each trade. These could be other mutual funds, hedge funds or individual traders with their own investment philosophies, which might have nothing to do with the "passive" philosophy of index funds. They can be divided into simple speculators and hedgers.

Hedgers

"Hedge" means to avoid commitment, and index funds are the largest source of speculative bets on Wall Street. In financial jargon, they are called "exchange-traded derivatives," "index futures," and "options," among other things. So, for example, a stock market might create a derivative which works as follows: the derivative is a bet taken on whether an index fund will rise or fall. Now let's say you bet $1 that X index fund will rise, and you place your bet. The market will then leverage your $1 into another $9 by taking loans out based on it. Therefore, in the end, you have a $10 bet on the index fund rising – effectively the same as a $10 investment in the index fund itself. The downside of these plays is that they are riskier; if things don't work out, you're leveraged for $9, and you need to pay it off. But if they do work out, you can earn a multiple of what you have initially wagered. According to the CME Group, the operator of the world's largest options and futures exchange, by far their largest equities derivatives products were all index products. Within this category, by far the most heavily traded index were futures and options contracts on the S&P 500 index.

To give you a little taste of hedging operations in action, I would like to tell you a story of a Japanese corporate treasurer for one of the biggest banks in Japan. I interviewed him about his experiences during the time of crisis in September 2008. His personal account is breathtaking.

Between 02:00 and 03:00 on Saturday, September 12th, 2008, rumors that Lehman Brothers would be filing for bankruptcy on Monday reached Tokyo's many banking HQs. The still young banker in the treasury department was summoned to the trading floor at once. He arrived in jogging pants, sneakers and a polo shirt, his hair ruffled from his sleep. At once, he was taken aback by his team's state of sheer panic. In a hectic emergency meeting, the bank's senior traders were ordered to hedge as much of their securities portfolio as possible – no questions asked. If they over-hedged, that wouldn't be a problem at all. They would be sharing their hedging positions with all of their affiliates in their banking network – the typical Japanese corporate culture to help out group companies in need. They proceeded to sell the heck out of S&P futures and everything that could be shorted for a decent price. From the vivid description my Japanese banker gave me, his index finger must have been running hot from pressing the sell button for index futures or purchasing index put options. In the end, his trading team was able to amass a giant hedging position foremost based on S&P 500 futures and options that helped the bank to weather the storm over the coming weeks and months.

So, who were the losers in this trade? Well, you might have guessed it: index fund owners and new buyers. Without them, there wouldn't be the liquidity in index funds, the stocks they contain and the financial derivatives that rely on them for their own pricing.

Speculators

Mark Spitznagel, owner and investment manager of the multi-billion dollar hedge fund management company Universa Investments, L.P., has a very interesting trading strategy that won't have much competition any time soon. His investment strategy, called "fat-tail trading," specializes in tail risk. This is the strategy made famous in Michael Lewis' *The Big Short*.

Tail risk is "a form of portfolio risk that arises when the possibility that an investment will move more than three standard deviations from the mean is greater than what is shown by a normal distribution."[39] Don't worry if that made no sense to you — what it means is that you develop a strategy by betting on really unlikely things, such as Bear Stearns collapsing in 2007 or Lehman Brother going the way of the dodo. Most people are unwilling to bet on such an event; they can't even grasp this possibility. But as the supreme innovator in bet making, Wall Street made it possible. Some out there bought these exact bets, and they made a killing. Spitznagel specializes in purchasing these types of bets and makes fortunes in the process. He is not your traditional investor, but a speculator who utilizes the systemic flaws of the financial system and their players to his advantage.

Unlike the typical player, Spitznagel is willing to lose a bit every month — and for a couple of years in a row, if necessary. Then, he usually makes a killing on one big event, such as Lehman Brothers going bankrupt, Greece causing trouble for Europe, or flash crashes. Not a lot of investors are willing to lose a bit month after month, only to wait for the big payout. And guess what the core building blocks of his bets are? *Index derivatives contracts*. It's not a closed and insulated world out there for index fund investors — they are all part of a much bigger ecosystem. For every action, there is an equal and opposite reaction.

Everyone Wins – Right?

Bogle himself perfectly summarized the strengths of index funds: "maximum diversification, minimal cost, and maximum tax efficiency, low turnover [trading], and low turnover cost, and no sales loads."[40]

After reading the part about the bright side of index funds, you should have a good sense of all the advantages index funds have to offer – for all parties involved. In short, "passive" investing can produce *market returns* for a fraction of the cost of actively managed mutual funds. With that, they are able to outperform more than 80% of all mutual funds.

We can boil these down to two basic advantages:

- Minimal cost
- Conceptual simplicity

Retail investors can certainly profit from the existence of index funds – after all, the history of mutual funds has not always been kind to them. As Bogle always envisioned for his index funds, it would become the people's road to participating in a new world of owners' capitalism and shareholder democracy – fair capitalism for all. Clients are assured that they are saving and participating in the fruits of capitalism. Index fund providers are also happy, as their asset size continuously rises, and as we know, their growth powers the entire Wall Street food chain. But we do have to remember that there are still losers. There always are.

DAVID SCHNEIDER

PART TWO
THE INDEX FUND MINEFIELD

DAVID SCHNEIDER

Chapter 4
PROBLEMS OF THEORY AND PRACTICE

Assumptions are the things we don't know we're making.
– Douglas Adams

As we have seen, index funds and index ETFs can be a very potent investment vehicle for the average investor. John Bogle, in his The *Little Book of Common Sense Investing*, explains the advantages of this particular mode of investing as follows:

> "Simply by buying a portfolio that owns the shares of every business in the United States and then holding it forever. It is a simple concept that guarantees you will win the investment game played by most other investors who—as a group—are guaranteed to lose."[41]

For Bogle and his entourage, it's a simple decision: Buy index funds. Keep buying index funds. Then, sit back and profit!

Unfortunately, the simple truth is that all financial products and their touted strategies have their flaws, and that includes investing in index funds. The flaws that are related to index funds can be divided into three major groups. The first is related to the theories that underlie index funds. Then, there are problems associated with the actual buying and selling of index funds – what I like to call "problems of execution." Lastly, there are problems related to the way index funds end up working, and the behavior of their buyers and sellers. We will see that even Bogle looks with some concern or outright criticism on recent developments in the industry he has fought for all his life.

In this part, we will look at these flaws and other major criticisms of index funds and index fund investing. Keep in mind that this list is not aiming to be comprehensive; it is just a summary of the most relevant flaws any index fund investor needs to consider before, and while, investing in index funds.

Issues of Theory

Some of the theoretical flaws underlying index fund investing are so technical that you could write a PhD thesis simply analyzing them. The most critical flaws lie in the assumptions index funds and their projected performance are based on. Let's look at the underlying assumptions of index fund investing by looking at the attitude of the index fund camp one more time. Bogle writes:

> "Simple arithmetic suggests, and history confirms, that the winning strategy is to own all of the nation's publicly held businesses at very low cost. By doing so you are guaranteed to capture almost the entire return that they generate in the form of dividends and earnings growth."[42]

If you read between the lines of Bogle's introduction to index funds, you can quickly identify the unifying theme of his strong beliefs – the idea, in the long run, that stocks always go up. If we further dissect this core belief, we can identify a few more assumptions that lie beneath it all. Bogle writes, "The returns earned by business are ultimately translated into the returns earned by the stock market."[43] For this to be true, we need to assume the following:

- Market participants are rational
- Market prices reflect reality – hence markets are efficient
- Risk rewards fair returns in the long-term

Hence, index investing theory states that market prices reflect financial reality at the company level, asset prices fully reflect all available information, and hence markets are efficient. Among economists and financial experts, it is called the *efficient market theory* (EMT). By implication, efficient market proponents and index fund investors argue that it would be useless and futile to search for market inefficiencies or even try to beat the markets in performance.

For the efficient market theory to work, all participants must be deemed rational. This, in turn, must mean that all market participants must be efficient allocators of capital. Companies with good earnings will then rise in price, while those with bad or negative earnings will fall in price, because the masses of all participants with all available information know and act accordingly.

Economics, unlike math, physics, or chemistry, is not an exact science, no matter how much people wish that it was. Famed financial journalist Henry Hazlitt noted:

> "Economics is haunted by more fallacies than any other study known to man. This is no accident. The inherent difficulties of the subject would be great enough in any case, but they are multiplied a thousandfold by a factor that is insignificant in, say, physics, mathematics or medicine - the special pleading of selfish interests."[44]

Standard economic theory assumes that human beings are capable of always making rational decisions and that markets and institutions, in the aggregate, are healthily self-regulating. It's a fine assumption, if you believed in a world of efficient markets.

However, economist Richard Thaler makes a pretty devastating observation: "Conventional economics assumes that people are highly-rational – super-rational – and unemotional. They can calculate like a computer and have no self-control problems."[45] You can immediately see a problem here: how can people be rational 100% of the time? Are you? Is anyone you know? If these assumptions could be true, we wouldn't experience losses, bubbles or crashes, and markets would be in constant equilibrium. We all know that that's just not true. So, what does that mean for market prices, if markets are neither efficient nor their players rational?

The Tyranny of Prices

There is nothing more important to index funds and their holders than today's market prices. The reason is simple: the main determinant of your performance in index funds is the average purchase price of all your past purchases. If the average purchase price of all your purchases is lower than the current market price of the index fund, you can account for a book gain. The reverse is also true: if the index price moves lower than your average purchase price, you will need to account for a book loss.

There were periods where stock markets as a whole performed very well for an extended period of time – so-called bull markets. Annual returns were positive with very rare downturns (which were followed by quick recoveries). Just buying some blue chip companies in 1980 could have gotten very respectable returns until about the end of the 1990s. A good year would bring double-digit returns, and in a weaker year, you would make at least a little. However, these magic periods always coincided with a massive stock market bubble, e.g., the US from 1949 to 1956 or Japan from the late '70s to late '80s. Afterward, years of satisfactory performance get completely wiped out by one market correction of

30% or more.

To demonstrate a quick example of this pattern, let's assume you bought an S&P 500 index fund a couple of years after the dot-com bubble burst, because you felt reassured by Greenspan's expansionary monetary policy. You bought the S&P 500 at around 1,000 in the summer of 2003. Year after year that follows, you experienced great performance, and with each passing year, you bought more of your index fund at higher prices. Well, why not? It had worked out for several years in a row, and you didn't want to miss out with your remaining money being dormant at low-interest rates thanks to Greenspan. Then you entered 2007, and by March 2009 your index fund traded at below 900, about 10% less than what you initially bought it for. Unfortunately, you bought successively more at higher prices, so the real losses were actually much higher than just 10%. All those years of great book gains are gone in one disastrous year with maximum impact. And now you are presented with a classic *investor's dilemma* – risking more losses or holding out and hoping for a miraculous comeback.

With hindsight, we know the answer to that today, but many investors bailed with maximum losses. Academics are still trying to find answers as to why we repeatedly follow the same destructive cycles. It certainly doesn't help that investors seem to willingly contribute to rising market prices like zombies in search of brains. A team of behavioral economists showed that when investors in retirement plans earn high returns, making them richer, they increase their saving rates, most likely because they extrapolate this investment success into the future.[46] This behavioral pattern has not changed, and even in 2017, we see this same pattern in full swing.

The main issues with standard index funds are that market prices have been known to vary a great deal. Equity markets have been known to experience prolonged financial Ice Ages, called bear markets. (Japan is still experiencing this, decades after the collapse of their housing bubble.) If prices are high, all will be well and you feel great; if prices are low, your performance will have a real impact on your financial planning. The projected performance of an index fund is just a theoretical one-time record, generated once a year based on data from the beginning to the end of a calendar year. In short, it is entirely dependent on the overall health of the market, which is unpredictable.

Second, although stock prices may have nothing to do with the actual success of the underlying businesses, they are easily accessible and highly visible quantifications of market opinions. Though everyone knows, on some level, that market prices are the result of a million variations that may have nothing to do with reality and the tangible world, they still fixate on price quotations as a meaningful reflection of their success. This can lead to disappointment and long stretches of time where an investor's patience is tested to the core.

Again, Japan is a very good example, of a country where companies within major stock indices have improved their profitability, rapidly expanded overseas (especially in Southeast Asia, the fastest-growing region in the world), and have become much more attractive on any accounting basis since the great Japanese real estate and stock bubble of the late 1980s. Yet the market prices are still below any rational valuation metrics. Neither local nor foreign investors seem to be particularly interested in Japanese stocks due to their collective mistrust of Japan's economic future. Horrific demographics are often quoted as the most popular excuse – yet most of the leading companies in any Japanese stock index generate an ever-increasing portion of their sales and growth overseas. On occasion, the health of the market is actually irrelevant to the actual value of the stocks in it.

Third, there is more to market prices than meets the eye. Market prices are not as objective as most of us want to assume. Prices reflect not only economic concepts, but the collective psychology of all market players combined, and it's this collective psychology that can be manipulated. There are many parties that have tried and achieved success to various degrees.

Thus, we see that prices don't follow the theoretical course that academics and index fund proponents would like us to believe. However, what does that mean for the risks you take when investing in financial markets?

The "Risk = Reward" Fallacy

In the world of professional money management, risk can be measured in mathematical terms. They start by taking historical price movements, known as "price volatility," as their point of reference. Volatility is defined as historical price fluctuations that can give a meaningful indication of how much a stock's price will vary in the future. Based on this, professional money managers feel confident making statements along the lines of "X investment will pay returns of X.X% over X period." The more volatile a stock has shown to be in the past, the riskier it is considered to be in the future. However, riskier bets also have greater potential earnings. If we take on additional risk, so economic theory argues, we are, like clockwork, also compensated with an equal amount of returns. When applying risk specifically to equity index funds, such as the S&P 500, there is what financial experts call an "equity risk premium." It is defined as "excess return that an individual stock or the overall stock market provides over a risk-free rate."[47]

When investors take on more risks, they want to be compensated for it appropriately. Taking on equity risk is substantially more risky than the "risk-free" rate of US government bonds. As we all know, the US government promises to return all principal lent, and some interest on top of it. Equities don't make any promises at all. Hence, they need to compensate for that uncertainty.[48] The size of the premium can vary, as the collective understanding of risk among market participants varies depending on where we are in the economic cycle. Some clever people concluded that if we all took higher risks, we are automatically compensated with higher returns – otherwise financial markets would be irrational. This was wonderful, because it enticed masses of investors to take on riskier investments in the hope of higher returns.

However, the core problem is this: if price volatility of the past is the main determining factor of risk today, you automatically make an assumption that prices have been properly assessed by efficiently working markets and by rational, honest market participants throughout the time records have existed. Furthermore, you assume that prices going forward will do the same. Anyone who has lived through the Asian crisis of 1997, the Russian default crisis, the dot-com bubble or the colossal subprime crisis from 2007 to 2009 must admit that this just isn't true. What if markets simply priced in too much risk or too little, as they have in the past? We as investors will not get compensated appropriately for that. The distribution of risk and fair returns is not a linear relationship. You might take on too much risk, not being aware of it, and pay for it in the long-term as markets slowly adjust price/risk anomalies, leaving you with years of unexpected underperformance.

In fact, if you go out right now and read any document which uses standard deviation as a meaningful measure of financial risk, you'll see the small print tells you precisely what I've previously written. Standard deviation, or historical price volatility, is a "guide" only, and that market movement is "unpredictable."[49] Unfortunately, this information should be what people read first and pay attention to, but the sophisticated marketing mechanisms of Wall Street and beyond have reduced it to size eight font at the bottom of their glossy portfolios. In short, assessing and utilizing price volatility, as a gauge for financial risk, is only a tool of many, but over-reliance is a fool's game, as all the financial disasters of the past have proven so vividly.

The "Markets Always Rise" Fallacy

A core assumption of the entire mutual fund industry is that market prices always rise in the long-term. And in a way, there is no arguing with that. If you had invested in the first publicly available index funds in 1976, you would have made a decent annualized return after accounting for inflation. In the summer of 1976, the Dow Jones traded at around 1,000. In January 2017, it was trading at around 19,900 (not inflation adjusted).

The problem with this is that economies and world affairs constantly change, which doesn't allow all of us to keep our wealth. The assumption is just plain unrealistic (for most of us).

The problem is that "rising" prices are dependent on the time frame we are operating in. If we measure performance from 1976 to 2016, performance looks very good. However, from 2000 to today – not so good. From March 2000 to March 2009 – pretty awful. In this last phase, you will see that the nominal value decreased from about 1,400 to 900, representing a loss of about 35% for ten years of patient waiting.

Returns based on potential capital gains in the future, rather than real cash flow income, have always been volatile. One day you can show off a sizeable book gain; the next day, you keep quiet because now you have to account for a book loss. Let's face it – markets have never gone up in a linear and predictable fashion. We have seen periods of stagnation and long periods of falling prices in the form of massive Ices Ages. These come and go. The question is: how long are you willing to wait?

Overweight, Underweight

Have you ever considered how indices themselves are constructed? As we have seen, index makers, such as S&P Dow Jones, wield a substantial amount of market power. If a stock is added or dropped off an index list, it necessarily has an enormous impact on the company's reputation and prospects. Even the mighty S&P 500 undergoes constant changes and adjustments. According to a study by Jeffrey Wurgler, a professor at NYU Stern School of Business, the S&P 500 index undergoes 20 to 25 changes in an average year as companies are added and removed from the index.[50]

Who defines what a proper index is, and what it is not? As of now, there are no global standards nor a committee of general benchmark assessments. So any financial corporation or any mutual fund company can create (and has created) their own lists of indices for various asset classes.

This issue may seem irrelevant until you consider that not all stocks within an index are equal. Most reputable index funds mirror benchmark indices that are structured as *market-weighted indices*. This is another way of saying that the bigger the market capitalization of a stock is, the more influence it has within the index. So if Apple, one of the largest companies in the S&P 500, booms, the price of the entire index goes up. In other words, the index is disproportionately influenced by a large stock such as Apple, Microsoft, or Exxon. That means that if any of these giants experience some form of crisis, you as an S&P 500 holder will also feel the pain, even though the index is made up of 500 US companies.

This has drawn much criticism from parties that argue that their own way of creating indices is more beneficial and delivers better returns. One side effect of market capitalization is that popular industries are always overweight. A good example of this is the boom years of tech and internet stocks in the late 1990s. As internet stocks moved up in price, they flooded major stock market indices. As a result, all indices became more heavily weighted in an overpriced sector. The S&P 500 and Wilshire indices were heavily weighted in companies such as Cisco and Enron, versus old economy stocks such as Exxon and GE. Conservative investors who bought index funds for the balanced diversification they offer were indirectly drawn in by the whole madness of the dot-com bubble. The heavily tech-weighted Nasdaq Index lost over 70% within two years, while general market indices such as the S&P 500 lost more than 50%.

The same phenomenon happened when banks, subprime lenders and homebuilders were heavily overweighted in all major stock indices at the peak of the housing bubble. As we all know, it didn't end well for the entire financial industry, and there were waves of bankruptcies and government bailouts. Again, all index fund holders disproportionately suffered under the folly of one market sector. Again, major indices such as the S&P 500 lost more than 50% in the wake of the subprime crisis.

As Joel Greenblatt, famed investor and author of *The Little Book That Still Beats the Market* observes, "This is the exact opposite of what an investor should want." Investors should not be overpaying for assets that could cause substantial losses to their invested capital, especially if they are aware of overpricing and market booms. That's investing 101. Yet in index fund investing, we are encouraged to do exactly that."[51] What he concluded was that with any bubble, market cap-weighted indices will always over-represent the industries that cause a bubble in the first place. Index fund holders would always suffer the consequences of such market anomalies more than they actually deserved or even wanted.

Recently, a growing camp of experts has argued for a new type of indices. The strongest group in this camp favored "fundamental indices" as opposed to standard "market cap-weighted indices." This means they preferred indices that consider accounting and valuation measures, such as P/E ratios or P/Book ratios, over simply choosing stocks weighted by their market capitalization. Famous proponents like Joel Greenblatt and Robert Arnott, academic and former editor of the renowned Financial Analyst Journal, are in this camp.

Arnott argues in the March/April 2005 edition that his newly designed "fundamental index" is superior to traditional market cap-weighted indices.[52] In it, he proposed weighting companies by their actual fundamentals, such as book value, sales, dividends, and cash flow. Such weightings, he believed, would more closely approximate the "true" intrinsic value of companies, rather than the popularity as measured by, at times, irrational crowds of investors and inefficient markets. When WisdomTree Investments launched its first 20 dividend-weighted exchange-traded funds in June 2006, CEO Jonathan Steinberg called market cap-weighted indices "flawed." Naturally, Steinberg argued that his new ETF

"...had the potential to change the way investors think about indexing and investing."[53] Modesty was never a strength in the financial industry. However, here starts the problem of fundamental indexing. The camp itself is divided.

All fundamental index proponents claim they have developed new methods of weighing portfolio holdings, which would outperform traditional index portfolios. Unfortunately, for that camp, individual proponents cannot seem to agree on a standardized form of building fundamental indexing. Where Greenblatt claims he has found the magic formula, Arnott has his own index composition.

Not surprising, John Bogle has always been a critic of "fads" disguised as "new paradigms." In a 2006 contribution to the op-ed pages of The Wall Street Journal, he wrote:

> "[W]e need to be cautious before accepting any "new paradigm" that implicitly suggests that the "old paradigm"-reflected in more than $3 trillion of capitalization-weighted index investment funds- is in error,"[54]

Capital, Capital, Everywhere

One of the main critical points of index fund investing is the matter of inefficient capital allocation. Consider what would happen if, in fact, everyone did invest only in index funds. James Stack, a widely respected investment newsletter editor and money manager, suspects that it could have some serious repercussions. In a recent edition of his *InvesTech Research* letter, he warns that so much indexing of stocks can raise market volatility, reduce portfolio diversification and exacerbate losses into a protracted decline.[55] The problem, as he sees it, is that the advantages of index funds on the way up become serious drawbacks when the market reverses course.

John Bogle himself thought about this issue and concluded

that a market dominated by index funds would be "chaos without limit. You cannot buy or sell, there is no liquidity, and there is no market."[56] If you think about it, if everyone was passively invested, no one would be buying and selling stocks. The basic purpose of the market – to move capital to where it's required – would cease to operate. At current levels of index fund activity, this is fine. True anarchy, says Bogle, "would require indexing to grow immensely from today's levels. Probably not until passive funds are at least 90% of the market could such chaos arise."[57]

Furthermore, if everyone puts his or her money into index funds, wouldn't their money inflows create colossal overvaluations of the stocks in the indices themselves? Prices are made up of immediate demand and supply realities. If there is less supply than demand requires, prices must necessarily rise. So as various index funds grow in popularity, so will their price. If everyone wants a piece of the Vanguard pie, you can rest assured it will end up costing way more than the actual value of its ingredients. In short, it'll be overvalued.

Professional money managers are getting more and more nervous of "the increasingly distorted levels of the valuations of some of the largest index funds." The combination of a prolonged bull market and rising popularity of passive investing has helped all stocks rise in value. Norm Alster of *The New York Times* writes, "Stocks that might not be bought singly on their own merits have been lifted by the package buying."[58] One fund manager interviewed for that article notes, "There's no doubt... that passive investing in ETFs and index funds inflates the price of index stocks versus non-index stocks." Brian Frank – a traditional active fund manager for the Frank Value mutual fund – asserts, "The whole market is overvalued [and] index stocks are more overvalued."[59]

Hence, the main criticism leveled by active fund managers at passive investing is that they constitute, in effect, "inefficient capital allocation." Passive capital markets cannot possibly allocate capital efficiently. According to Inigo Fraser-Jenkins at Sanford C. Bernstein, index fund investing could become so incompetent in allocating capital that in some ways, it is worse than the Soviet era when the USSR's economy was hamstrung by massively inefficient and cumbersome bureaucracies.[60] Soviet leadership, at least, aimed at allocating capital according to a grand plan to spread the influence of Communism across the globe. Index funds, on the other hand, aim to make money simply by assigning their cash to particular – already successful – corporations, and riding their coattails to riches. This goes against the very purpose of an efficient capital market, which is to provide liquidity where it is needed, when it is needed, and to whom it is needed.

Moral Hazards

Yet another side effect of inefficient capital allocation is a topic that relates to CSR – corporate social responsibility. With broad and compulsive diversification and mechanized systems of allocating capital, there is always the possibility of investing in ethically dubious enterprises without buyers actually being aware of it. Certainly these days, there is an increased awareness of ethical issues associated with companies with negative headlines – witness the recent outcries over Walmart's dubious compensation strategies and SeaWorld's use of killer whales. Issues of climate change, gender equality, exploitation of Third World countries, and fair animal treatment have all come to the fore. Many have realized that not addressing these issues simply makes for bad business.

Since the subprime crises, there has been a worldwide outcry against Wall Street, its leading institutions, and a few individuals who seem to pull the strings of high finance. No corporation has been targeted more than Goldman Sachs. This is tricky, because, Goldman is part of *many* reputable benchmark indices. In fact, Goldman Sachs and other financial corporations like it, made up about 16% of the S&P 500 index in 2016[61] – second only to the IT sector.

Many of my liberal friends and acquaintances have been openly demonstrating or boycotting certain companies and products for years. The majority are very eager to convince others to join their good cause. However, when I ask them how they feel about the latest index fund contribution, and I point out that they themselves are the biggest financial backers of the same companies they are so feverishly boycotting, the reaction is universally surprise and horror. The bottom line is this: when you buy into an index fund, you sometimes have no idea what kind of corporations you're buying into.

It's up to individuals to decide for themselves how they manage their investing matters in keeping with their values; in addition, they should be aware of moral inconsistencies and the support they may be unknowingly giving to the very people they consider the "bad guys."

Issues of Practice

Here's a truth that shouldn't surprise you: the practical execution of buying and selling and rebalancing the portfolio of an index on a continuous basis is much more work intensive and complex than a phrase like "mirroring an index" might suggest. Come up with some arbitrary rules (e.g., no companies with red in their logo, no companies founded between 1945 and 1965), and try to find thirty of them. Then, set limits for yourself (e.g., buy if their stock goes up by over 1%; sell if it declines by more than 6%). Now try to buy all these thirty stocks and track them on a daily basis, adjusting them as and when needed. Pretty soon, you'll see how complicated it can get.

Now imagine you do that for 500 stocks at the same time or, even 4,000 stocks. On the scale at which major indices work, any major trade can move market prices and change liquidity for each stock being traded. In the case of Apple, every day, millions of shares are being traded; in the case of the smallest company within the S&P 500, it's a fraction of that.

In the same *Bloomberg News* interview, Gerry O'Reilly (Senior Portfolio Manager at Vanguard, who oversees more than $800 billion) gave a brief description and tour of Vanguard's operations.

O'Reilly's main job is to make sure that the $450 billion Vanguard Total Stock Market Index Fund matches the performance of its 3,600-stock benchmark. What makes his job challenging is the constant inflows and outflows of their funds.[62] When money is in surplus, he must invest that money immediately according to the composition of that index and vice versa. Not so easy if you have a 4,000-stock benchmark to mirror.

When it comes to index funds, all of this leads to *issues of execution*. Let's take a closer look at some of them below.

Tracking Errors

Most indices need some sort of supercomputer and trading algorithm to figure everything out. Moreover, this is what the index industry and the mutual fund industry have invested in: massive IT infrastructure. All this complexity means that there is still lag in keeping up with market movements. With all the computer prowess and sophistication of trading algorithms in the world, it simply isn't possible to copy any index with 100% accuracy, 24 hours a day. In short, index funds will never be able to exactly mirror their selected indices, even though they have continuously gotten closer. The remaining residual lag will always remain, and among experts, this small gap is called a "tracking error."

Furthermore, most index funds offer daily liquidity, which means that any investor can take their money back at any time. All the adding and withdrawing of money complicates things, especially the management of an index fund. If you have too much cash not being invested, and the market rises, you underperform; if there is not enough cash available, the manager will have trouble meeting its financial commitments, which would require ad hoc selling with the risk of influencing market pricing in more illiquid stocks.

To make up for this tracking error, index fund operations have found additional sources of income by lending out their shares for a nominal fee to short sellers. What does that mean? It just means that you give an outside party, who bets on falling prices, permission to bet against positions in your fund. Short sellers who speculate on falling prices usually take short positions in stocks that they think will fall in price. To set up their bets, they need to borrow the stocks in question. In any bet, parties require some form of collateral, and borrowing stocks guarantees delivery when the punt is over. Lending stocks to short sellers has always been an additional source of income for index fund managers. They have never seen harm in the fact that others are actually betting against their own position within their portfolio. Hey, what can a single short seller do to harm the entire index?

Left Out in the Cold

In a world where market capitalization is the key factor of stock benchmarks today, companies with a larger market capitalization experience a disproportionate flow of trading activity in their shares, making it much easier for those companies to raise fresh capital at favorable conditions through stock issuance or bond finance. Keep in mind that this quirk goes back to the issues of market cap-weighted indices. Companies not included in a specific index don't get buying attention from countless index funds. These companies have a much harder time raising capital from markets; it's usually at less favorable financial terms, as there is less demand for bonds or stocks issued from those companies. The rich get richer.

However, it is not only the capability to raise fresh capital at better market terms, but also how management could behave under the cover provided by their index fund shareholders. "Companies that can rely on a regular flow of capital are, to a large extent, sheltered from market conditions. This results in the rise of what specialists identify as a 'lack of incentive to guard against risk.'" [63]

The money invested in these giant funds is allocated in accordance with the benchmark index they mirror. The companies that create the indices, however, have very different aims and goals than investors. Corporations in that favorable position might have less pressure and fewer incentives to act in the best interest of their shareholders. They may be tempted to initiate unnecessary share buybacks at overvalued prices, mergers, and acquisitions that don't make economic sense, along with other bad economic decisions – all under the assumption that the money will keep coming in. According to Eelke Heemskerk, a political science professor at the University of Amsterdam: "If you have only long-term investors, how do you keep management on their toes? Where are the checks and balances when you have such large block holdings?"[64] This goes into another criticism for index funds – that of corporate governance.

If all investors in their company were index funds, who puts real pressure on them, as an index fund's only mandate is to mirror an index? If the company is in an index with a special market cap weighting, the instructions for index fund managers are clear: buy and mirror that weighting.

On the other hand, people outside of the index simply get less attention and less favorable capital market terms than those companies on the inside – starting from less liquidity in their stock as all the trading action happens with companies inside an index. Even worse befalls companies that are booted out of indices. When all giant index funds are pushing the sell button at the same time, you can assume that their stock prices will plummet.

This issue is exacerbated with index funds that track the value of bonds issued by countries – e.g., 10-year US Treasury bonds. Indices will automatically include more bonds of countries considered more "reliable" – such as the US, Germany, and Japan. In turn, this means that these countries have more and more people buying their bonds. In effect, a country like the US can issue more and more debt, because they have a large amount of money coming in. Conversely, less reliable nations, like Costa Rica or Thailand, for example, struggle to secure liquidity regardless of how well their economies are growing. It's no coincidence that American debt is ballooning while countries like Malaysia seem to have much healthier current accounts.

Some professionals argue that this fundamental flaw of indexing and the wide adoption of know-nothing investors is the main reason why we are experiencing one of the largest debt bubbles in the history of finance, with bond prices rising for seven years straight. Bond markets, in general, have been enjoying a bull run for an incredible 35 years. By 2015, the debt market had swollen to $76 trillion – what many experts believed was certain bubble territory. It is powered by debt issued in countries such as the US, Germany, and Japan.[65] Yet, none of that seems to matter for bond index funds, as they continue inflating said bubble.

Checklist Governance

Providing money to debt issuers or becoming shareholders doesn't only come with rights, but with important responsibilities – one of which is corporate governance. At the annual Daily Journal meeting, Charlie Munger, co-chairperson of Berkshire Hathaway, expressed concerns that the rapid rise of index funds was having a negative impact on this, too. "Index funds," he argued, "will be permanent owners who can never sell. That will give them power they are not likely to use well."[66] Other leading active managers, such as Mario Gabelli, have pointed out that index funds weaken corporate governance due to their passive nature and primary mission to simply reflect, and not guide, the performance of a market index.[67]

Both make good points. According to Heemskerk, the two largest index fund managers, BlackRock and Vanguard, already own at least 5% of more than 2,600 companies worldwide. Funds run by Vanguard alone hold roughly 6% of total US stock market value. That's a lot of voting power in the hands of only two fund companies. Recently, both fund providers have been very public about their involvement in corporate governance. According to a recent Vanguard interview, "Given our size and stature, we are an important voice today in corporate governance matters, and vote to the sole benefit of our mutual fund shareholders."[68] At the beginning of 2016, BlackRock's Larry Fink sent an open letter to chief executives at S&P 500 companies and large European corporations to emphasize how important an issue of corporate governance is to BlackRock.[69]

For all their power, in the past, both rarely voted against or held incumbent management teams to account. Critics of index funds point to what Warren Buffett called the "checklist approach" to corporate governance, as evidence of their invidious influence. As a result of not having the time nor the resources to look through each and every company in detail, as would be required to fulfill their responsibilities as major shareholders, index funds tend to reduce their understanding of their wards to checklists and simplistic metrics. Their mission is not to govern companies within their index but to mirror an index performance as closely as possible and at the lowest fee possible.

Other critics refer to a more serious issue related to conflict of interest. Both Vanguard and BlackRock are eager to gain corporate pension fund schemes as their clients, but no self-respecting executive is interested in putting employee savings under the control of money managers who might be overly aggressive and vote against them at the next annual shareholder meeting. As a result, critics claim, it is very rare for institutional money managers, including Vanguard, BlackRock or State Street, to vote against company boards, even if they are highly doubtful about a particular course of action.

Chapter 5
PROBLEMS OF PARTICIPATION

> *The inherent irony of the efficient market theory is that the more people believe in it and correspondingly shun active management, the more inefficient the market is likely to become.*
> — Seth Klarman

In the last chapter, we had a look at some of the more technical flaws of index funds. In this chapter, we will take a look at how we are supposed to make use of index funds – at how index fund proponents and providers prescribe index funds to retail investors. As we shall see, the fund experts and money managers are very much divided as to how we should deploy our cash. They also fail to agree about shortcomings of their investment approaches, their theories and assumptions, and what the consequences are for us. These all constitute what I like to call "issue of participation" – in other words, problems that arise from the way people are told to participate in the world of index funds.

Not So Simple

You might have heard the standard advice for getting into index funds – open an account at Vanguard or any other leading index fund provider and simply buy one big market index. To refresh your memory, the advice according to Bogle: "simply by buying a portfolio that owns the shares of every business in the United

States and then holding it forever. It is a simple concept that guarantees you will win the investment game played by most other investors who—as a group—are guaranteed to lose."

In the same camp as Bogle are JL Collins and Mr. Money Moustache; both are famous financial bloggers who swear by keeping it very simple with index funds. On his blog, Collins argues that what "any of us really need are two of Vanguard's funds: VTSAX (Vanguard Total Stock Market Index Fund Admiral Shares) for our stocks and VBTLX (Vanguard Total Bond Market Index Fund Admiral Shares) for our bonds. This is, after all, The Simple Path to Wealth." Mr. Money Moustache concurs, but adds: "Just a single Vanguard index fund is the simplest thing you could do, which would be buying the VTI exchange-traded fund and that just gives you the entire US stock market." He added a further option by including the VXUS, the ticker code for Vanguard Total International Stock ETF – "You can do a little better. Very small amount better if you mix VTI and VXUS. That's another Vanguard fund. Then keep them balanced with annual re-balancing 50/50."[70] However, in practice, it is rarely as simple as "just buy one and sit back." Following is a story from J.L. Collins' blog that illustrates just how confusing the process of buying an index fund can be.

One of his subscribers followed his advice and swapped actively managed funds for index funds, and moved her assets over to Vanguard. Thanks to her substantial asset size, she was entitled to a free consultation with a Vanguard representative. She was surprised that there even needed to be a consultation for a product that was marketed as "buy and hold one single S&P 500 index fund." As she progressed, what she heard from Vanguard baffled her even more. She got a list of six different index funds – all Vanguard's – she was supposed to buy for her new account, all with different Vanguard ratings, weighting allocation ratios, and fee charges. According to her own account, the Vanguard contact person did not even explain the rationale of this elaborate portfolio composition, but just referred her to the online form she had filled out. Needless to say, she was not only confused but pretty irritated.

As an intelligent person, she wanted to know how her money was being used, and why. The Vanguard representative couldn't provide her with the basic information she was hoping for.[71]

One of her questions: How do you know which fund is best? If you're supposed to buy one which covers the whole market, then right off the bat you'll have a choice of not tens, not hundreds, but thousands – and each is pitched as the best by those who own them. In the US, there are more than 100 index funds that mirror the S&P 500 alone. If you visit Vanguard's website, you can find out that they offer an entire suite of low-cost index funds (across multiple types of asset classes). BlackRock and State Street also have their own growing family of index funds and ETFs. Beyond that, there are more than 4,400 ETFs worldwide, with most of them mirroring indices.[72] As previously mentioned, in 2016 alone, over 240 ETFs were launched – again, most of them mirroring indices.

Here's another question: Why should it necessarily be a US benchmark? Under the patronage of John Bogle, popular consensus among financial bloggers is to focus only on US benchmark funds. Bogle himself swears by the S&P 500 or US Total Market Index in all his books, because the leading US companies already engage in global trade. General market consensus would agree that future economic growth is going to be in Asia and other emerging markets and that the Asian region, in particular, will enjoy higher growth rates over the next 20 to 30 years. In this regard, some clever investors have been quoting Walter Gretzky, father of hockey great Wayne Gretzky: "Skate to where the puck is going, not where it has been." Thus, we should be betting on the future growth of Asia rather than maturing economies of the US, Europe or Japan. Conversely, if you've put all your eggs in Basket USA, you'd be entirely justified in scratching your head over the current state of the US economy, and the new President who is famous for his many spectacular bankruptcies.

You can see we can play this game ad infinitum, without being much closer to the answer of which index fund or ETF to buy, and in what proportions we should buy them. It will remain a highly subjective process without any guarantees of success. In the end, each investor has to decide for him/herself how to allocate his/her money. To do that with confidence, there is no alternative but to get involved – in other words, *invest actively*.

A Dollar Here, A Dollar There

You might have noticed that in the story of the woman who went to Vanguard, one of the sales techniques the rep to whom she spoke used was to propose several funds with different fee rates – leaving her completely in the dark about how much she'd be paying, and for what. In fact, Vanguard's index funds offering can vary from less than ten basis points for a simple S&P 500 index fund to 40 basis points for a more exotic index fund, such as the Vanguard Emerging Markets Stock Index. Furthermore, not all index funds are low cost and not all index providers charge the same low fees. Consider the S&P 500 Index: the mother of all indices is tracked by more than one hundred different funds, all attempting to replicate its performance in very similar ways. Yet, they charge different fees from a few basis points to over 100 basis points.[73]

Tony Robbins argues that mutual funds are cheating you on expense ratios. According to him, traditional mutual funds charge 80 to 100 basis points, but at the end, you are presented with a bill of, on average, more than 300 basis points.[74] How is this possible? Well, these charges are bulked up with fees, charged before you even start investing; sales commissions and promotional activities; third-party fees that could range from administrative to legal fees; extra charges associated with entering or leaving an index fund – and so on.

Something very similar happens to buyers of index funds from various providers other than Vanguard. If you open a bank account, you will be charged fees for all sorts of administrative expenses. Maintaining accounts for keeping your index funds might also cost you. Your index fund itself might charge you only the expense ratio as indicated in their sales prospectus, but you still would need to pay your annual dues for holding those funds in separate accounts and all those third-party services that you can read up on in the small print of your fund advisory contract. There are fees for account services, purchase and redemption fees, and other transaction costs that could accumulate. Some less morally inclined index fund providers have even sneaked in fee structures that mirror those of actively managed funds.

It does catch up with the funds, eventually, but never on a scale that seems to affect their business. One of the more pesky issues for BlackRock has been a string of lawsuits over fee complaints. Claims have been brought forward that their fees are far too high, especially when compared to their contemporaries in the same field who offer the same service for much less. At least, that was the claim of the Florida lottery winner who invested his winnings in BlackRock mutual funds – and what's more, he also argued that BlackRock ended up charging him far more than what they said they would.[75]

Another disgruntled customer complained about being overcharged for withdrawing his money.[76] Yet another group of shareholders filed lawsuits that claimed that over a span of three months, BlackRock overcharged them without any explanation or warning. In other more complex cases, several subsidiaries of BlackRock were being accused of mishandling pension funds that were held by BlackRock. The main complaint here was that pensioners who put in their money expected a decent return on their 401(k) or IRA. What they received instead was not even close to the projections, even with supposedly safe and non-volatile investments like plain index and mutual funds that were sold as safe.

BlackRock claimed that it had the right to charge more, as the funds they bought required more active management. Apparently, they didn't just buy plain simple index funds or their shareholders simply didn't know what they were buying in the first place, assuming they were simple index funds. Whatever the case may be, BlackRock's string of lawsuits, combined with many other legal cases brought against different index fund providers including Vanguard, illustrate three fundamental issues with their clients and the products they bought.

- Clients regularly underestimate the real fees involved even for index funds
- Clients are confused by the product variety of today's index fund universe
- Clients have unreasonable return expectations induced by over optimistic advertising.

Certainly, there are big differences between index fund providers and how they disclose fees to their clients, but that doesn't excuse the fact that the whole industry is not very much different from the traditional mutual fund industry. Your only comfort might be that traditional mutual funds still charge more than you are being charged for holding a portfolio of index funds and exotic ETFs.

Asset Allocation, or, How to [Not] Stay Wealthy

As Tony Robbins noted in *MONEY Master the Game*, "Anybody can become wealthy, but asset allocation is how you stay wealthy." Almost all investment books, financial advisors and bankers preach the same gospel of asset allocation and risk diversification. With data meticulously collected from institutional money managers, they argue that performance is much more dependent on which asset class you put into your portfolio, rather than the individual securities or fund selection within each asset class. In other words, if you bought stocks right before the dot-com bubble burst, the best stock or fund selection would have been meaningless – you would have experienced losses either way. You should have kept (allocated) more money in bonds and real estate or simply held cash.

In hindsight, this is an obvious conclusion. The theory behind it is that when owning or "allocating" your money to a set of asset classes, it can protect investors from the ups and downs of individual asset classes while still being gainfully invested. Index funds are ideal for this, as they offer the cheapest way into a multitude of asset classes. Furthermore, if you own all possible assets at the same time, ideally spanned over the entire globe, it will enable you to participate in any hot asset class around the world. If Chinese stocks are hot, you will have some exposure; if oil or gold is hot, you will have some exposure.

However, here's a question – how do you know how much money to allocate to each class of investments? In what exact ratios are we, the average individual investors, supposed to know to structure our individual portfolio? If you Google "asset allocation," you'll come across something that looks a lot like this:

Example of an Asset Allocation Model with Index Funds

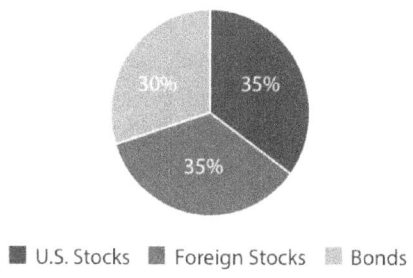

■ U.S. Stocks ■ Foreign Stocks ■ Bonds

This is the sort of structure Tony Robbins describes in his book as the "All Weather" portfolio. It is a specific asset allocation model he based on extensive interviews with professional hedge fund managers, such as Ray Dalio, who calls his strategy "All Season." Dalio is the founder of the investment firm Bridgewater Associates, one of the world's largest hedge funds with around $150 billion AUM. "All Seasons" may sound harmless, but in effect, Dalio and his firm make most of their performance from the stupidity of other market participants who don't play the game as well as they do.

However, copying a world-renowned hedge fund manager is not easy, and Robbins himself is pretty skeptical about the possibility of success for others: "Many of the replicas were down as much as 30% or more in 2008."[77]

While pooh-poohing the competition, using the term "fake Rolex,"[78] Tony endorses his own set of portfolios, simply naming them "All Weather" portfolios.[79] With all the fancy naming, financial professionals dismiss the "All Weather" asset allocation approach as "nothing more than a cookie-cutter, bond-heavy asset allocation."[80] .." Moreover, this is not the only inconsistency we find in Tony Robbins' quest to help his fans achieve financial independence, while at the same time collecting generous fees for his financial services.

In his book *MONEY Master the Game*, Tony Robbins states, "What I have known from the beginning is that success leaves clues. People who succeed at the highest level are not lucky; they're doing something differently than everyone else." He certainly didn't make his fortune conventionally, i.e., from saving parts of his income and putting it in index funds. According to Forbes, Tony Robbins was estimated to be worth $480 million as of 2015. He made his fortune by being a rather outspoken entrepreneur relying foremost on his personal strengths – excellent self-promotion and an ability to inspire others. Over the many decades, he has built a well-diversified media empire that includes several income streams, and which is now tilting more and more towards financial services.

Still, he uses the same investment platitudes that the mutual fund industry has been promoting since 1924. It's the same conventional advice that has been given in the financial industry since the dawn of time: Buy a bunch funds (on the cheap), imitate some elaborate asset allocation model, and hope that the "magic of compounding" takes over. For these services, the companies he endorses will charge you to the tune of 1.5% in fees annually. The world of money has always been filled with extreme paradoxes.

While we are talking about bond heavy asset allocations, if you're thinking, "Well, bonds are safe, right?" think again. Though places like the US and Japan seem 100% safe, both have their own economic travails, and Japan, in particular, could blow up at any moment. The United States debt ceiling crisis of 2013, and the current state of the US national debt, certainly do not instill confidence in investors. The recurring congressional spending crises are certainly a good reminder to US debt holders of what could happen if the US ever shuts down.

So, then, what if we have just enjoyed a long, bullish phase for debt instruments? Before Lehman Brothers filed for bankruptcy on September 15th 2008, more than $3 trillion was invested in money market funds according to *The New York Times*. The FED and the Treasury, under the leadership of Paulson and Bernanke, obviously forgot that Lehman was the dominant player for short-term money market products such as Commercial Paper (CP) – funds usually considered to be of the highest quality. When Lehman Brothers went bankrupt, panic broke out, forcing the government to intervene and restore confidence in global money markets. Nevertheless, some of the so-called "safe" money market funds lost money when writing off commercial paper issued by Lehman Brothers.[81]

All right, you say – I'll keep all of my savings in cash! But even if you only kept cash, you would still have to deal with the possibility of losses – either in the form of inflation eating your hard-earned money away or the profit opportunities wasted. If you kept your cash in various currencies, you would have to deal with daily price fluctuations. These days, currency fluctuations are so extreme among the leading world currencies that you could easily gain or lose 15 to 20% against another currency – a terrible thing for most conservative investors.

If you're tempted to just throw your hands up in the air and say, "Fine, I'll just leave it to the professionals," think again. Even the professionals mess up big time in an almost predictable fashion – as can be seen from the example of the *target date fund massacre of*

2008. William A. Birdthistle, Professor of Law at Chicago-Kent College of Law, conducted an excellent study on this incident in his book *Empire of the Fund*.[82]

Target-date funds hold about $800 billion in assets, including 15% of all 401(k) assets. Their particular growth since 2006 is also the result of receiving the highest honors any mutual fund can get: "appropriate Qualified Default Investment Alternatives (QDIAs) under the Pension Protection Act of 2006." QDIAs are funds that a 401(k) plan fiduciary may choose as a default investment for all their workers.[83]

As the name suggests, target date funds are structured around a specific target date – specifically the date a client intends to retire. They are typically structured as funds of funds. That is, the target-date fund holds investments only in other mutual funds, rather than in securities. So, while a typical mutual fund might feature a portfolio of stocks or bonds issued by hundreds or thousands of different corporations, a target-date fund might invest in a mere handful of other mutual funds. Indeed, the most rudimentary approach would be for a target-date fund to invest in just two other funds: an equity fund and a bond fund. Vanguard's 2055 fund invests in four other funds: one US and one international equity fund, and one US and one international bond fund, similar to the standard recommendation of index fund purists.

The investment advisors that offer target-date funds include years in their titles. The idea is that a person who turns thirty years of age in 2015 and who plans to retire at age sixty-five would choose the Target Retirement 2055 fund. Throughout those decades, the fund itself — and not the investor — make the prudent adjustments from holding primarily equity investments to primarily fixed-income investments as the target date approaches. This change in allocation over time is known as the fund's "glide path." The manager of the fund adjusts the fund's ratios. Thirty-five years before the target date, for instance, the fund's manager might allot 70% of the portfolio to the underlying equity fund and only 30% to the underlying bond fund. Over time, the portfolio manager would slowly shift from more equity to more bonds until the fund reached almost all cash or very liquid assets, as the target date neared. The rationale behind this is to reduce market risk as the planned retirement approaches, and cash withdrawals are more likely.

On paper, all would be fine, but reality never plays by the rules. The real first test for target-date funds came in the aftermath of the 2008 financial crisis. The official figures displayed a fiscal bloodbath minus 40%. As The New York Times reported: "People in their 60s and late 50s, with funds dated 2010 and 2015, were flabbergasted that their accounts had lost a quarter of their value, on average, as calculated by Morningstar, the fund research service."

A shock for investors. A fund just a mere two years away from its target date ought to have almost completed its conservative glide path – bonds and cash almost entirely. This alone should have been protection enough against any price decline of the 2008 stock market disaster. So, what was the reason for such epic failure? *The New York Times* gave a blunt explanation of why those funds unveiled horrendous losses: "These funds typically had about half their holdings in stocks, and most of them did not significantly reduce that percentage until the investors were in their 70s or older."[84] Americans live longer after retirement, hence terminal funds saw themselves justified to have higher equity proportions generating more capital gains and potentially more income. Another reason mentioned was that equity index funds, particular overseas versions, charge higher fees and bring in more profits for the investment advisor as a whole. It's difficult to prove which reason was responsible for such a disaster, as what remained were losses for those who could afford it the least.

DAVID SCHNEIDER

Chapter 6
PROBLEMS OF NARRATIVE

Religion is about turning untested belief into unshakable truth through the power of institutions and the passage of time.
   – Richard Dawkins

If you study the world of index fund investing, you will over and over again read and hear something along the lines of "index investing represents a superior investment strategy, and everyone should use index funds as the core of their investment portfolios" (Burton G. Malkiel Princeton), or "...superior returns [are] achieved by the index fund" (John Bogle), or even "The Power of Passive Investing lays out an irrefutable case for buying low-cost passively managed index funds and ETFs."[85] All of which would be true, if it weren't for one major fly in the ointment: the majority of people who invest in index funds lose money.

In this chapter, we will discuss the biggest flaw of index funds and passive investing: the matter of the "recurring loser." Even though proponents claim superiority over all other mutual funds, the sad fact is that index funds haven't changed the face of stock market investing, the mutual fund industry, or the investment world in general. We still have boom-and-bust cycles; we still have plenty of fraud; and we still have the majority of investors losing out due to the consequences of this.

In a recent blog article, the editors from

brokenleginvesting.com made some bold statements about the typical index fund investor: "Most investors fail at it. Academic studies have shown, and anecdotal evidence confirms, index fund investors don't achieve the buy-and-hold returns advertised by funds like Vanguard."[86] There is plenty of evidence to back up this rather depressing observation. According to marketwatch.com, the average holding period of an equity mutual fund is about 3.3 years, and for a bond mutual fund just 3.1 years.[87]

Peter Lynch, former manager of the actively managed Magellan Fund at Fidelity Investments, confirmed these observations in his book *One Up On Wall Street*. In his own estimates, two-thirds of the people who invested in Magellan during the time he managed the fund lost money as a result of the sort of behavior previously described – even though he generated a staggering 29% average return during his 13-year tenure as manager. DALBAR, one of the leading industry research firms, noted: "Over a 20-year period, December 31, 1993 through December 31, 2013, the S&P 500 returned an average annual return of 9.28%. However, the average mutual fund investor made just over 2.54%."[88] Again, that includes both actively and passively managed mutual funds. It shows that the average index fund investor doesn't really utilize the key advantages of index fund investing – the 1% to 2% cost advantage, and possible better long-term performance over all other funds.

Index fund proponents often mention the intellectual superiority of index funds and those who buy them. They are supposedly more sophisticated and advanced than investors in funds with active management, just by association. Unfortunately, there is no evidence that buyers of index funds, especially ETFs, are more sophisticated than those buying traditional mutual funds or even simple stocks. Past statistics of inflows and outflows for index funds prove that the average index fund investor behaves the same as any other ordinary mutual fund investor. When economies boom and market prices rise, index funds experience disproportionate money inflows. It stops when the market tanks, followed by massive money outflows. It seems that all the benefits and rational arguments are lost on their average client, with only a minority being able to follow through. Hence, Bogle's vision of an "ownership society," capitalism for the masses, hasn't panned out so far. I'm sorry to say that it never will pan out unless the entire industry (including Wall Street) and their clients fundamentally change.

In the following paragraphs, we will look at the reason this is so. The answer lies in three key factors: the nature of index funds themselves, the psychology of their buyers, and the incentives offered to index fund providers.

Index funds – A Disguised Bet

Not too long ago, I interviewed a hedge fund manager who uses a very quantitative approach to trading financial securities. I asked him his opinion about index funds and the answer he gave surprised me: "David, index funds are bets! Awful bets, with terrible odds. You could make 5[%], but eventually, you'll lose 50[%]." I was ready to argue with him – until it struck me that managers and owners of hedge funds or any money pool are rarely on the losing side of the grand bet. It's their investors who take real risks, pay the fees, make bets, underperform and suffer the consequences. This got me wondering – how come? Are index funds really just plain money pools whose mission it is to copy the "natural" movements of an index?

To understand the true nature of standard market index funds, we could approach this question from a different angle. As you might know from Economics 101, our economy is broadly defined as a provider of goods and services and the supply of money. So, where do mutual funds – or more specifically index funds – fit in?

Are index funds products or services? Not really. A service is defined as an "action of helping or doing work for someone." If you go to a language school, take classes of any sort, or even get professional advice on matters of a legal or medical nature, there are strict objectives, aims and outcomes. It either works or it doesn't. You either receive something of real value, in the form of expertise solving a particular issue, or you don't and you move on. One could argue that index funds make us rich and deliver on what they promise. But – first – they don't promise anything, and second, they simply can't deliver, or we all would be rich by now. They simply provide broad market exposure at low fees. It could be debated whether this is really a service that creates value for its clients if they experience losses of 50% or more.

Are index funds providers of capital? Again, not really. No mutual fund is a current medium of exchange in the form of coins and banknotes, nor are they a good storage of value, as gold could be considered. You are not providing capital directly to any companies in an index. As Bogle himself noted in a recent interview with Bloomberg, "The stock market has nothing – n-o-t-h-i-n-g – to do with the allocation of capital. All it means is that if you're buying General Motors stock, say, someone else is selling it to you. Capital isn't allocated – the ownership just changes."[89]

What can we infer from this? Index funds just don't fall in any of those traditional categories that define our economy. So, if they are neither physical goods, money, nor services, what are they?

As you might recall from Chapter 2, when you buy index funds you buy shares of a mutual fund. As mutual fund expert Birdthistle writes, "A mutual fund investment (...) is an equity arrangement. That is, fund investors are shareholders, not creditors nor account holders; they hold stock, not debt."[90] The consequences of this legal status are important, because they permit substantial – even total – loss in the investment. If what you "own" goes down, you don't have recourse to claim anything back, because technically, you don't own anything but a claim on an imaginary pot of money, and if that pot shrinks – tough. Here lies the fundamental danger of all index funds – they are not risk-free.

As Bogle noted:

> "[index] funds eliminate the risk of individual stocks, the risk of market sectors, and the risk of manager selection, with only stock market risk remaining (which is quite large enough, thank you)."[91]

What Bogle touched on is called "equity risk premium." We should know by now, and from your own experiences over the last 16 years that real markets just don't follow the perfect models of economists. Since 2000, we have experienced two declines in US equities markets of more than 50%. If you were concentrated in equity index funds and had no other allocation to bonds, real estate or cash, there wouldn't have been any other alternative than to deal with these declines. However, it doesn't stop at equities. The same goes for any other major asset classes, including so-called "safe" bonds, commodities or real estate purchases. All of them can – and will – experience similar price declines in the future and from the looks of it, most likely at the same time.

So, what does this all mean? Well, the bottom line – and the single most important thing for you to remember about index funds – is this: *When you purchase standard benchmark index funds, you purchase a "bet" – you're betting that the index prices will rise.* Granted, the bet might have a higher propensity to pay off the longer you hold it, but in the short-term, you will have to deal with the entire range of possibilities inherent in any price bet, including massive declines.

As we all know, the line between investing, speculating and gambling is a fine one, especially when we deal with Wall Street. In the end, prices are the main determining factor of your future profits. If you buy a US index fund, you make a bet on rising prices in the US, and furthermore, you make a bet on America – a bet on its business and industrial, political and financial systems. Then again, there is nothing wrong with making bets, especially if it is on such patriotic causes as betting on your country. However, more naïve fund buyers convince themselves that they are grand investors in the businesses of corporate America. They are not! Neither are they providing capital nor are they really aware of what goes on, on an operational level of 500 companies or more.

Index funds are the very epitome of playing Wall Street. You are making a price bet on the entire market that is controlled and powered by Wall Street. However, like in any bet, bets can go either way – they're the ultimate psychological challenge. And so we come to my next point, which is that in addition to essentially being bets, index funds also have a very particular psychological impact, which further multiplies the number of people who buy in – and then cash out at the worst possible time.

Psychology be Damned

Imagine you are a passenger on an ocean liner in the cold and dark northern Atlantic – and the ship just hit an iceberg. As the vessel begins listing to one side, the captain tells everyone that the only way to survive is for all the passengers to move to one side of the ship and stay there. Anyone who leaves for the rescue boats might have a higher chance for survival individually, but as soon as the first person jumps over board, it would seal the fate of the entire ship and everyone onboard. However, if they stay onboard, and the captain's plan doesn't work, they're sure to drown.

What would you do if you were faced with such a dilemma? More importantly, what do you think everyone else would do? The index fund industry has long settled on their answer – stay on the damn ship. They tell you that you can be a winner, but only if you overcome your instincts and follow the advice of the mutual fund industry to stay for the long-term or, in Bogle's own words, "Stay the course!" Unfortunately, hardly anyone seems to be listening. In the past, investors bought into stocks and funds as they were rising, and then, in market corrections, sold at very inopportune moments. They would take their money out and wait until the fund went up before buying again – the very opposite of the cardinal rule of investing: "Buy low, sell high." As index fund proponent

Charles Ellis, author of The Index Revolution, confirms: "The sad result is that investors time and again buy after a fund's best results have been recorded and sell out after the worst performance is over."[92]

It's believed that our daily lives are largely determined by our insecurities and psychological misjudgments, especially when the topic of money is involved. Nobel Prize winner Professor Daniel Kahneman of Princeton University researched how decisions and mistakes are made. According to Kahneman, "If we think that we have reasons for what we believe, that is often a mistake. Our beliefs, wishes, and hopes are not always anchored in reasons."[93] In his studies, Professor Kahneman and his late colleague Amos Tversky realized that we have two systems of thinking. With their research, they opened a new branch of economics called behavioral economics. What they described was a world where our decisions and judgments are a result of a battle in our mind – a battle between deep-rooted instincts that manifest themselves through our intuitions.

Seth Godin, the famous marketing guru, refers to this as the "lizard brain." It controls our intuitive reactions and daily decision-making. It has evolved over millions of years into a very powerful control mechanism. According to Kahneman, "our thinking is riddled with systematic mistakes," known among psychologists as cognitive biases. "They make us spend impulsively and be overly influenced by what other people think. They affect our beliefs, our opinions, and our decisions, and we are not even aware it is happening."[94] Add the *investor's itch* (the impulse to be active because you might lose out), and you can see that we have a very interesting cocktail of powerful psychological forces that causes various forms of cognitive bias. When it comes to making decisions regarding money and putting it to work, it seems that our lizard brain too often takes hold of us, and with some very dire consequences.

One of the most interesting examples of psychology and investing converging is the aforementioned significance of price quotations, and the dramatic psychological feedback loops these can cause. They have been a never-ending source of psychological torment for generations of speculators, investors, CEOs, and economic policymakers. Prices impose themselves directly on our psyche. If you've ever found yourself checking your phone for price quotes several times a day, for something that should matter in 10 or 20 years, you'll know what I'm talking about. Those already invested feel stimulated to invest more at higher prices, as they might be thinking of all the gains they are missing out on with their dormant cash at more or less 0% interest.

On top of all this, there is a familiar behavioral pattern when playing with "house money" – money from previous successful years – that isn't part of the initial investment. In real gambling, the matter of general risk aversion quickly fades when punters gamble with house money. The same behavior pattern can be observed in financial markets, where people take more and more risks at higher prices as they feel they won't lose their original investment – that the money they're playing with is somehow "bonus cash." As Richard Thaler writes in his book Misbehaving: "The house money effect – along with a tendency to extrapolate recent returns into the future – facilitates financial bubbles."[95]

Let's look at recent trends. Since 2007, according to national surveys, the rate of households owning stock, through direct or mutual fund investments, has gone down from over roughly 65% to around 55% in 2015.[96] Not surprisingly, the rate improved somewhat from a low in 2013 of 52%, and it seems to be gaining momentum.

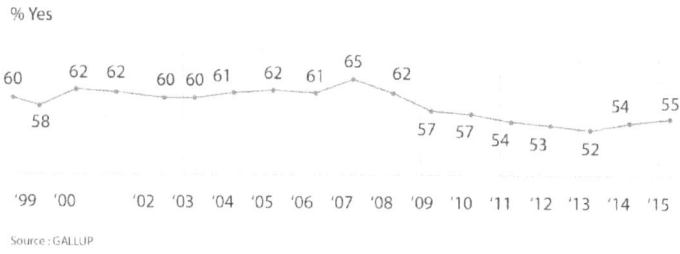

People who missed the rise in the stock market over the last five years were pressured to play catch up and jump on the indexing bandwagon. As a result, since March 2009, the S&P 500 increased more than 200%. According to Morningstar, in 2016, index funds experienced fund inflows of $625.2 billion, actively managed funds posted outflows of $92.3 billion, and the Dow Jones breached the 20,000 mark for the first time in its history.[97] "One would do well to remember that this state of affairs is not a new phenomenon," warns Steven Bregman, co-founder and president of Horizon Kinetics, an independent research firm specializing in inefficient markets. "In prior eras, it was known as go-go investing, or trend following. Now it takes the guise of index-based asset allocation."[98]

In fact, experience shows that most people didn't invest in stocks until the rally was in its final innings. At the start of 1982, only $41 billion of the $241 billion in mutual funds was in equity funds; the remainder was in bond ($14 billion) and money market ($186 billion) funds. By the end of 1990, assets in bond ($291 billion) and money market ($498 billion) funds still outnumbered assets in stock ($239 billion) funds three to one.[99] Only by the end of 1996 did assets in equity funds exceed that of their debt-oriented cousins. From this, it is fair to infer that many individual investors who dove into the stock market did so near the height of what was then a bubble, and probably enjoyed only a few years of solid returns before the 2000 crash. The same pattern had emerged before the subprime crisis brought the next rally to an end. After 2000, post the dot-com bubble disaster, equity ownership immediately dropped. Eventually, it reached a new high at over 65% at the peak of 2007, just before the housing market collapse.

It doesn't help that the majority of investors have very idealistic return expectations of their index. Most pension funds in the US still expect 8% or thereabouts, according to a McKinsey Global Institute report published in 2016. The report states that customers expect "returns typically in the 7.5% and 8% range for a portfolio of stocks and bonds." The conclusion of this report is that institutional investors and retail investors need to reduce their investment return expectations.

As Lewis Brahams, author of *The House That Bogle Built*, tactfully described it: "A similar pattern of the ignorant herd of investors stampeding into overvalued asset classes at the worst possible moment has recurred throughout history – from the eighteenth century's Dutch tulip bulb craze until today's housing bubble." Part of the blame lies in the index funds and their providers, who have created a system of perpetual marketing that works almost too well in absorbing new capital – and in compounding the potential impact of a potential collapse.

Blissful Ignorance

Warren Buffett is often quoted as saying, "By periodically investing in an index fund, for example, the know-nothing investor can actually outperform most investment professionals. Paradoxically, when 'dumb' money acknowledges its limitations, it ceases to be dumb."[100] The instructions are simple: Put your money into index funds regularly, and don't touch it. Index funds will take the hard work and complexity of investing away, and work their magic spontaneously. No future crisis will matter because in the end the market always rises. This would be fine advice, if we behaved like all the economic models assume – robot-like!

Advertising tells you to trust in past statistics, Nobel Prize winners' endorsements, and higher prices in the future. They also point out, however, that past success is no guarantee for future performance. It's OK to be "dumb," to be a "know-nothing" person in the game. However, there remains another crucial problem – we as consumers don't learn anything, except how to transfer money from ourselves to our money managers and our financial advisors. Index funds might be easy to understand and transparent in their concept, but only a few experts know what really goes on behind the operations of a multi-trillion industry. For the rest, it's a black-box.

In any financial crisis, you neither will have learned the mechanics of investing nor will you be prepared for the logical consequences of boom-and-bust cycles. You won't even know whom to blame for your miserable financial situation. Try to sue any of the mutual fund providers, and you'll discover it's pretty much impossible. A good example of how dangerous the "know-nothing" approach can be is the way *"dollar cost averaging* (DCA)" ends up working. Let's say you've just landed a cushy new job, and you go to the Oracle of Omaha – Warren Buffet – for advice on what to do with your extra monthly $1,000. His advice is simple: Periodically, buy index funds. Just like your good friend LeBron James, you should "just make monthly investments in the low-cost index fund"[101] This sort of regular monthly investment is called "dollar cost averaging."

Why averaging? Well, this technique (which some claim Benjamin Graham himself, who taught at Columbia Business School from 1928 to 1955 but who never practiced it himself) is basically "diversifying across time." The argument goes that because timing is impossible (since we don't know where the bottoms and peaks are), it is wiser to just keep on buying on a monthly basis. According to a standard definition of DCA, "Essentially, an investor places a fixed dollar amount into a given investment (usually mutual funds) on a regular basis. The investment takes place every month regardless of what is occurring in the financial markets. Time pickers cannot forecast the direction of the market because they cannot know the next news story. There is no competitive edge that exists other than illegal inside information. The best way to earn the market's fair return is to simply remain invested at all times."[102]

The idea behind this is that while an investor purchases more shares when prices are low and fewer shares when prices are high, the average share price is automatically lowered over time. So when the markets are up, you'll pay $500 for, let's say, 50 shares of Big Corp. When they're down, you'll get 100 shares for the same dollar amount invested. So between the two purchases, the average price for 150 shares in total evens out. Tony Robbins advises: "You don't want to hesitate to get in the market trying to have perfect timing; instead, use dollar cost averaging and know that volatility can be your friend, providing opportunities to buy investments cheaply when the market is down."[103]

According to experts, DCA is "how you avoid letting your emotions screw up the great asset allocation plan you've just put together by delaying investing."[104] I am also very fond of this argument: "It's the key to sleeping better at night, knowing your investments will not only survive unstable markets but also continue to grow in the long-term, no matter what the economic conditions."[105]

So far, so good. Now, let's consider a worst case scenario: An investor dutifully starts contributing in a standard benchmark index fund of a reputable firm on a monthly basis. True to theory and expectations, the price of the index rises. Over the years, she has accumulated several dividend payments, which are plowed back in at higher prices. Then, disaster strikes. The index drops, and it drops a lot more – a full selling panic breaks out, as so many times before in the history of financial markets. The prices drop much more than the average purchase price of all the monthly purchases in the past. As it turned out, she increased the dollar amount of her monthly contributions over the years, with more purchases at increasingly higher prices. For the first time, she is presented with zero gains for all those years of saving (or with book losses). At this point, she lost the capital gains of the past and all the dividend payments she had accumulated and reinvested over the years. However, it gets worse. She loses her job. Not only does she stop contributing to her savings plan (which could considerably lower the average purchase price), but worse, she is forced to sell out of financial need. And so ends her foray into index funds and financial markets.

The point here is that even though she was invested in the markets – for a long time – because of the "know-nothing" nature of her investment, she had no idea what went wrong when things went wrong. In the end, dollar cost averaging, though convenient and recommended, robbed her of any understanding and opportunity to be engaged in her investment process. The tendency of many people in this situation is to simply bail, because trying to understand the market when it's tanking is simply far too stressful and far too depressing. As we see in any great slump, the majority of people just choose to take their money and run.

The 'Buy and Hold' Doctrine

We have already seen from previous chapters that index funds aren't perfect. The entire mutual fund industry is aware of this, but instead of capping return expectations and trying to speak some sense to overeager clients, they do the exact opposite. They encourage them to buy and hold, and add as many investments as possible, arguing not only that the indices will continue to provide outstanding returns, but that holding onto them in the long-term – and indeed expanding your position – is the only way to go. They are never tired of referring them to Bogle's own study on expected returns from his *Little Book of Common Sense Investing*. In March 2007, it was written:

> "Let's assume that corporate earnings will

continue (as, over time, they usually have) to grow at about the pace of our economy's expected nominal growth rate of 5 or 6 percent per year over the coming decade. If that's correct, then the most likely investment return on stocks would be in the range of 7 to 8 percent. I'll be optimistic and project an annual investment return (a bit nervously!) averaging 8 percent."[106]

More recent predictions show that he is being quoted as saying, "The S&P 500 should deliver 6% to 7% annual returns from 2015 through 2025 if the general stock market is fairly valued in 2025."[107] It is substantially less than before, but still too much for some research reports. A detailed study done by McKinsey tells us that these expectations are far too optimistic, and equity investors should be satisfied with less – much less. According to research by Star Capital, an independent private equity firm, the S&P's returns from current historically high valuations can be expected to be 4% annually for the next 10 to 15 years. In other words, no one seems to be able to agree on exactly how much index funds will return.

Despite the general concerns about uncertain future returns, retail investors are still driven en masse into investments through 401(k) plans, stock and fund promoters, and an array of more exotic structures at higher and higher prices. Central to their vision of the ideal investor is the "buy and hold." At its base is the sort of thinking you can find on investment advice websites:

> "The expected return of the market is essentially constant and positive. Therefore, investors who are out of the market for any period of time can expect to lose money relative to a simple and low-cost buy-and-hold strategy."

> "The best way to earn the market's fair return is to simply remain invested at all times in a

relatively low-cost, passively managed index portfolio."[108]

Just reading that makes me feel guilty for keeping cash in my bank account! To rob potential investors of any doubt, we can hear many success stories like the one John Bogle describes in his *Little Book*:

> "Celebrating the 30th anniversary of the fund's initial public offering [2006], the counsel for the fund's underwriters reported that he had purchased 1,000 shares at the original offering price of $15.00 per share—a $15,000 investment. He proudly announced that the value of his holding that evening (including shares acquired through reinvesting the fund's dividends and distributions over the years) was $461,771."[109]

The 30th anniversary was held in September 2006. Just two years later, Vanguard's legal counsel must have seen his 30-year investment cut by half in the midst of the subprime crisis. Keep this success story in mind when we discuss appropriate strategies for index fund investing.

Tony Robbins has his own little anecdotes to tell. One of his self-employed friends, who set up her own tax-advantaged retirement account with Vanguard, instructed the company to automatically deduct $1,000 from her bank account every month to distribute among her diversified index funds. According to him, "she's a long-term investor who doesn't worry about timing anymore, because her system is automated and the decision is out of her hands."[110]

The problem: Who has $1,000 a month to funnel into an investment account? The average US household income was $56,000 in 2015. This lady's investment rate would represent 22% of the average household's earnings – when in fact, most people can barely afford the average of 5.5%! Furthermore, that's a lot of blind faith – and money – to put into a scheme that might or might not work out. As we have seen, there is no conclusive evidence that index fund clients are any different from traditional mutual fund clients. In many cases, they are the same investors who just swapped their mutual funds from actively managed to passively managed funds. So why should today's index fund holders and buyers behave any differently over the next 10, 20, or 30 years? Why should index fund owners behave any differently in face of the next horrific crisis?

The fact of the matter is that the large majority of those invested in index funds today will lose money in the next downturn because they hold unrealistic assumptions and profit expectations, and constantly underestimate the psychological consequences of adverse market periods, which can sometimes last for decades. Here we come to one of the core problems of the index fund's "passive investment" doctrine: put simply, it entails all the risks of investing, with none of the ability to avert those risks through knowledge acquisition and understanding the nature of global financial markets.

However, why is "buy and hold" so important to the index fund world?

To answer this, let's begin by looking at the circumstances most "ordinary" index fund investors find themselves in before they enter the market. According to the annual study by NerdWallet, in 2016 in America "the average household with credit card debt has balances totaling $16,061, and the average household with any kind of debt owes $132,529, most of it coming in the form of mortgages."[111] This debt burden requires the average household to pay more than $6,000 in interest per year, which constitutes about 9% of the average income. In the age of total media coverage, we are constantly reminded of our retirement needs and bombarded with modern asset allocation models and sophisticated investment advice. The result is US households buy financial products that simply don't fit their financial needs nor their financial reality, which indirectly increases their financial leverage even more.

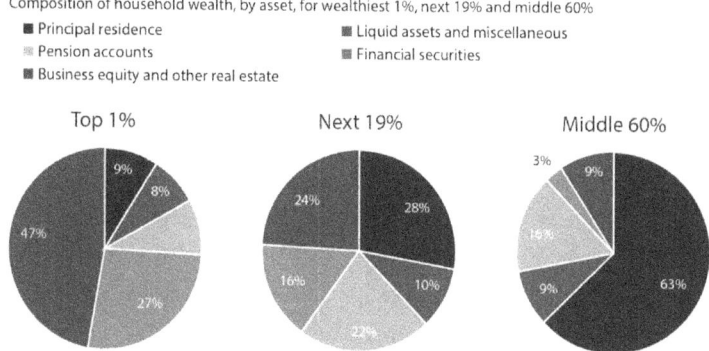

Asset Mix
Composition of household wealth, by asset, for wealthiest 1%, next 19% and middle 60%
- Principal residence
- Pension accounts
- Business equity and other real estate
- Liquid assets and miscellaneous
- Financial securities

Source: Edward Wolff, New York University

As ironic as it may sound, having the ideal asset allocation, as proposed by academics and financial professionals, costs money. You might have a house with a large mortgage, so you feel the urge to buy additional mutual funds, annuities or life insurance, all in the name of risk diversification. Alternatively, if you are already in debt and see markets run away, you might feel compelled to participate in the raging bull market. After all, your neighbors and the financial media are boasting of easy gains and future profits in the stock markets. Hence, you start investing in index funds, stocks and ETF products. This is, of course, all financed out of your monthly paycheck.

Let's assume the market tanks, the economy is forecasted to tank with it, and all the banks who wooed you in boom times are now getting nervous and are about to put screws on all your debt. What usually goes first are the things we can liquidate the quickest. The small cash reserves we nowadays have are quickly gone. What goes next are usually stock portfolios and even 401(k) plans with daily liquidity. Everything that ranks high in terms of liquidity in our personal asset columns will be turned to cash to fulfill pending debt obligations; nothing is more liquid than index funds and their ETFs. On top of that, you're selling at the worst possible time. You and millions of others start scrambling for the exits, which worsens the vicious cycle of falling prices. The result is that index fund investors and their counterparts in the traditional mutual fund camp experience the very same phenomenon that Peter Lynch and his clients experienced not so long ago. Some people will win in the long-term, but not until many more have lost in the short-term.

For those who run the index funds, this is an annoyance, but not the end of the world, despite the fact that many clients unnecessarily buy and sell their index fund holdings at the worst possible times. You'd think it would be bad for them if their customers did badly, right? Well, no. They continue on attracting new funds and new clients (from new generations with the same retirement concerns and similar lack of financial education, if necessary).

There had been estimates that by 2017, the investment world would equal about $17 trillion with roughly 30% belonging to index funds. As we know, the mutual fund industry can be divided into providers of actively and passively managed funds. Many times, the same mutual fund providers offer both under one roof in order to capture the growth on both sides. BlackRock, the largest asset manager in the world, as of the end of 2016, managed $5.1 trillion; this number goes up to $15 trillion[112] if we consider all of BlackRock's subadvisory contracts, which among others includes the US Thrift Savings Plan (TSP).[113] In 2016, they recorded total sales of $13 billion and net income of almost $4 billion.

However, it's not only the elites of index fund management that are on the receiving end. We have already seen that index funds and ETFs power entire industry sectors. They provide fees and commissions for lawyers, accountants, auditors, index providers and tech companies, which provide the technology and software that underlies a state-of-the-art IT infrastructure. Don't forget Wall Street and its armies of investment bankers and traders who live off brokerage commissions and market information. Hence, it might not be farfetched to say that vested interest is part of their industry existence, which could even go to the upper echelons of the political process through lobbying activities for financial deregulation.[114]

More than the mutual fund or hedge fund world, the index fund world lives and breathes by economies of scale. Hence, asset size matters in reducing operational cost relative to the size managed. Whether you manage one billion dollars or two billion dollars, fixed costs don't change. Variable costs are managed superbly, and profitability increases dramatically with each added billion. The more they manage, the more they can invest in technology, software, and key personnel, giving them a slight competitive edge over everyone.

Consider Vanguard, the largest mutual fund provider in the world, as measured by assets under management. According to the latest reports in December 2016, it commands roughly $3.8 trillion, which increases by about $1 billion in size every trading day.[115] It is the provider of the two largest index mutual funds, the $450 billion Vanguard Total Stock Market Index Fund (Admiral) and $240 billion Vanguard 500 Index (Admiral), which are only exceeded in size by the original and first index ETF, the State Street SPDR S&P 500 ETF. All this money helped keep costs low and continuously reduced the fees it charged clients – the so-called expense ratio. Vanguard today charges 0.04% for its institutional share class or, in other words, four basis points. Compare this to the original fees it charged in 1976 of over 40 basis points. A very impressive improvement, but unfortunately, that will leave them very little room for further substantial improvements. Fees can only be lowered so much.

These giants parlay their huge asset sizes into favorable terms with third-parties, such as brokers, legal, auditing, and administrative service providers. A big chunk of the operational cost is trading fees charged by brokers on Wall Street. Over the last two decades, the entire industry has been able to negotiate trading costs with brokers, as they have switched over to electronic trading and trade settlement systems. Companies have also created new kinds of financial products to encourage people to loosen their pockets, such as ETFs.

As we know, the first ETF was launched in 1993 by State Street. With the launch of the first ETF that was targeted foremost at retail investors, it openly challenged Vanguard for its retail index business. By March 2000, State Street had reduced the SPDR S&P 500's expense ratio to 0.12 percent, which was less than the Vanguard 500's 0.18% for individual investors at that time. By then, the ETF had already attracted $17.3 billion in assets.[116] John Bogle called them "the greatest shotgun ever made... great for killing big game in Africa, but it's also great for suicide." As soon as Bogle was out of the way, Vanguard would launch their own ETFs; today, Vanguard has 16% of its $3 trillion in assets in ETFs, and offers more than 50 ETFs. At present, some 65 million (!) shares of Spiders ($8.8 billion worth) are traded every day. The turnover of Spider shares runs at a 3,600% annual rate. The turnover for the famous tech ETF NASDAQ Qubes is even higher, at 6,000% per year.

So, in pursuing economies of scale, companies like State Street came up with products like ETFs. What does this have to do with the recurrent loser, I hear you cry? Well, as author Braham noted: "The problem is that because ETFs were designed to be traded, there is a temptation for investors to do precisely that, and at the worst possible times – buying hot ETFs at the top and selling beaten-down ETFs at the bottom." In 2015, John Bogle pointed out that the only "sure winners are the brokers and dealers of Wall Street."[117] As Braham noted, "It is a cruel irony that the index concept he helped champion has been exploited to create exchange-traded funds (ETFs) for speculators whose holding period can often be just a matter of minutes."

All this further reduces costs and boost profits, but in the end, companies still rely on the sheer amount of money under their control for the bulk of their earnings. In short, they need all those short-term "retail" investors. It doesn't matter if they pull their money out during bear markets – these companies will have squeezed as much profit out of them as they can. With their sheer size and influence, they can always persuade new investors or sit on their war chests and wait for the markets to turn.

The Passive v. Active Debate

Another core problem associated with the way index funds are advertised goes back to the work of academics in the 1970s, who first observed that "active" management didn't produce market-beating results. Critics responded by calling index funds "Marxistic" and "un-American"; defenders have responded by saying that passive investment is the "superior" and "only" form of successful investing.

For a variety of reasons – and whatever the truth of the matter – this whole discussion has, over the years, degenerated into nothing more than an extraordinary smokescreen – one of the biggest I have ever encountered in finance. As Mark Manson, famous blogger and author, described in one of his articles on marketing: "...if you can tap into people's insecurities – if you can needle at their deepest feelings of inadequacy – then they will buy just about any damn thing you tell them to..."[118] This is precisely what this debate does.

Fidelity, which initially was a fervent opponent of index funds and index investing, and Vanguard, whose early mission was not to manage money at all, offer a whole range of either actively or passively managed funds. So does anyone else in the mutual fund business who doesn't want to be left out of the asset-gathering bonanza. Here's the bottom line: the largest firms offer both actively and passively managed funds, and their ideological bickering has its limits as soon as they see their financial self-interest at risk.

Furthermore, the line between active and passive is extremely thin; what looks "passive" and seems like little work involves lots of active management. Consider what happened in 2002 with Vanguard's Total Bond Market Index Fund (symbol: VBMFX) when it underperformed the Barclays Capital Aggregate Bond Index (by a whopping 2%) and the index it was supposed to be mirroring to the letter. Here's Vanguard's explanation:

> "The fund trustees admitted to allowing the fund managers to use their discretion in the fund by making a large bet on corporate bonds—at precisely the wrong time—and then instructed them to sell the position, again at precisely the wrong time."[119]

Allowing managers to use their discretion? Weren't index funds supposed to track and copy indices to the letter? Clearly, there was some "active" management involved in this most "passive" of investment vehicles. The net result was a huge hit to investor returns.

So, it seems that there is some active discretion on how to manage "a passively managed" portfolio. If a company like Vanguard is enhancing their fund performance by trying to engage in the "passive" investment process, you can assume the whole industry is engaging in similar activities.

Conflicts of Interest

With the introduction of index funds, the money management industry experienced its own *disruptive innovation*. Initially, the whole industry was in denial, not ready for the abrupt challenges of "passive" investment. However, it adapted and learned how to coexist by creating business opportunities around it. They created classic cross-selling strategies, along the lines of "Want fries with your burger?" They created products that look like index funds, but charge high fees. Moreover, they flooded the markets with so many products that even professionals lost a clear market overview. The result is that index funds and all their auxiliary services are no less a fee-generating business than any other previous mutual fund operations. It charges its dues in advance and has been continuously growing over the last 40 years. Even though some older generations of fund managers still think of the "good old days," index funds have settled nicely into the money management world, and they are here to stay.

One problem that arises from the way the index fund world is organized is the intimate nature of links between different parts of the industry that should, theoretically, be independent of each other. The US Congress gave its own verdict on the unique relationship between many advisors and their funds in 1970, calling it "potentially incestuous."[120] Furthermore, some index funds are publicly listed firms, such as BlackRock. Foremost, don't these managers have a fiduciary duty to their own shareholders? After all, they have a board of directors themselves, and those directors are voted in by shareholders. Who comes first? Your shareholders who pay your salary and guarantee your job and retirement or your clients who are buyers of your products?

It was always John Bogle's criticism that the traditional fund industry "serves two masters" – the shareholders of the funds and the fund management companies. However, he seems to ignore that the same phenomenon might also apply to most of the index fund industry, just at a lower fee structure, which isn't even always true. What remains is the fact that an elementary conflict of interest remains, and this has been part of the industry since the first money pools appeared in the Netherlands and England.

No index fund provider is interested in reducing the inflow of money and reducing the selling of existing or new financial products, nor would they recommend staying away from certain asset classes that are riskier but yield higher profit margins for themselves. They would rather recommend adding new fund products, and promote ever more elaborate asset diversification and modern risk management models, which unsurprisingly come at higher fee charges. As William Birdthistle noted, "Fund shareholders benefit only when a fund actually generates investment gains; fund advisors benefit by increasing the assets under management any way that they can."[121] If this is through rising market prices, gaining market share or new customers, they really don't care, as long as their asset size continuously and consistently increases. If you consider who profits from your monthly contributions that come in like clockwork (DCA), it becomes clear who the real, consistent winner in the index fund world is. According to John Bogle, it's obvious: "Our financial croupiers always win. In the casino, the house always wins. In horse racing, the track always wins. In the Powerball lottery, the state always wins. Investing is no different."[122]

It's not just shareholders who stand to benefit; let's not forget the extraordinary compensation offered to the management of these firms. If we look at the salaries at the top of money management, we can see Bill Gross taking home $290 million in total compensation for 2013, just before he left PIMCO in 2014. It would seem he wasn't happy there anymore. Larry Fink, co-founder and CEO of BlackRock, was awarded $25.8 million in compensation in 2015, compared with $23.9 million in 2014. As of 2012, Larry Fink had an estimated $340 million. By 2016, it was certainly much higher. Robert S. Kapito, President at BlackRock, made $20 million in total compensation in 2015 (on top of a long line of similar compensation packages the years before).[123] The founding family of the privately held Fidelity is estimated to be worth $26 billion by Forbes magazine, which makes them the ninth richest family in the United States.[124] State Street Corp's Chairman, then CEO Ronald E. Logue, earned $28.3 million in total compensation in 2007.[125] State Street Corp's Chairman, then CEO Ronald E. Logue, earned $28.3 million in total compensation in 2007. Rest assured, the figures haven't changed dramatically for the new CEO in 2016.

Vanguard doesn't publicly disclose compensation plans for its top executives (that includes salaries and generous payments out of its partnership bonus pool). This is surprising for a company that prides itself on its transparency. They only state that they pay "competitive" salaries to key employees,[126] and we all know what competitive means in the financial industry.

Summary

Index funds are, as all financial products before them, not superior to other products but rather a financial tool for investors with their own unique characteristics, distinct benefits, and quirks. Index funds are neither superior nor evil. We need to keep in mind that index funds and their ETFs are just a form of mutual fund for various financial asset classes represented by an index. Because they don't do anything else than replicate an index, index funds themselves never make any outrageous claims, promise returns or give guarantees of any sort. Today, you can have index funds or ETFs for any asset class imaginable. The only limit on how far you can take the index fund game is the creative imagination of those folks working on Wall Street.

I am sure we will see an ETF on the price index of bitcoin very soon, as proposed by the Winklevoss twins. So, it's not necessarily the fact that you buy "index funds" that could put you at harm, but rather the asset class itself and the risk inherent to that asset class you buy through an index fund or ETF. If you buy bond index funds, you receive the collective returns of that asset class at probably the lowest cost possible. If you consider buying equity index funds, you are aiming to achieve equity market returns. However, you are exposing yourself to the financial risk of equity markets at a very low cost.

So the real issue is not with index funds or ETFs themselves, but how they are promoted and prescribed to the average retail investor with very little knowledge or experience about investing and financial markets. All the academic research and all the professional endorsements for index funds have created an aura of certainty and predictability. Constant growth is always awarded constant and fair returns. The whole index fund investing premise is that markets always rise, and you could be a winner, too, if you follow its rules. It suggests to the more naïve-minded that future returns come in like clockwork (over the long-term) and there is no additional effort or independent thinking necessary. Buying at any price and at any time is highly encouraged, and interfering with that money-moving process from your pockets to the industry is highly discouraged. In fact, it is considered harmful in the index game.

Unfortunately, the reality looks very different. The standard description of buying at any time, at any price and "holding it forever" is simply unrealistic. It ignores basic human nature and the flaws of today's financial markets that encourage speculating and frequent trading. It's simply unrealistic to think of the "long-term" if the average holding period for an equity fund has been less than 3.5 years. It doesn't fundamentally change just because we have switched actively managed funds with passively managed ones at low cost. The "holding for forever" premise is a farce if their buyers need their money back urgently in the next financial downturn or they see themselves seriously underfunded at the time of their retirement.

Then there is the matter of the industrial complex underneath the world of index funds that hasn't fundamentally changed. Even with the introduction of so called "low-cost" index products and endorsements from academics, the mutual fund industry is in control and highly profitable – just the names at the top might have changed. As a matter of fact, we can see the same symptoms of an inherently flawed and wrongly incentivized system creeping up again today. Product proliferation, hidden financial leverage, and gung-ho sales tactics that confuse retail investors are just a few issues we already know about.

Maybe you should realize that most index funds and ETFs are just another elaborate and disguised form of gambling your money away. Cheap bets powered by a collective imagination and hope of ever-rising prices and quick recoveries with constant average returns of 8% or maybe more in all eternity? However, bets are bets – they could go either way. In the end, index funds could be considered just another financial product to keep you in the big money game, as so many products and fads have before them. With any game involving big money and payouts, there will be guaranteed winners – the casinos – the facilitators and providers of games, and those few who constantly aim to rig the games. The index fund industry today is very much a part of this casino – the largest casino in the world.

Does that make index funds "un-American?" Certainly not! What could be more patriotic than betting on the leading US companies that dominate the capitalistic world? Are they the devil's work? Again, no. They are as good or as evil as sellers or buyers make them. Do they have advantages over the majority of mutual funds actively managed? Yes, they do. However, are they the perfect investment vehicle for the masses of retail investors and their retirement needs? So far, the results are mixed and less than conclusive. We will get a much better picture when generations of baby boomers start cashing in their savings and investment portfolios in earnest.

I would also add that it depends on how we use them. So, the conclusion is simple: how index funds are used and how passive investing philosophy is applied to a portfolio is the responsibility of the buyer. All this can be read in the fine print of any index fund and ETF prospectus (if you ever took the time to go through pages of legal jargon). In the final part, we do exactly that – take responsibility and take charge of how we should be using index funds to benefit only one party – you!

PART THREE
SOLUTIONS

DAVID SCHNEIDER

Chapter 7
Salvaging Indexing

Everything comes in time to those who can wait.
— Francois Rabelais

According to Morningstar, in 2016, index funds experienced fund inflows of $625.2 billion, and actively managed funds posted outflows of $92.3 billion. Since March 2009, the S&P 500 has increased by over 200%. This is a new record in index fund history. More and more advisors and professional promoters are promoting index funds in earnest. As more people invest in index funds, prices most likely go up. Now it has become a momentum play as success breeds success, as long as the momentum lasts. "The index universe has become a big momentum trade (or, perhaps, an interest rate momentum trade). It is the most crowded trade in the history of investing."[127]

Let me put my cards on the table: this peak is a bubble, and having a policy of not thinking for yourself and handing your money to someone else in the hope that something good will happen is foolish. You cannot rely on instructions from an industry that has its own financial agenda, no matter how tempting it may seem. Whatever the index fund or mutual fund industry lobby might suggest, you still have to think for yourself, as you alone will ultimately be held responsible for your investment decisions. So, before you consider putting a single penny into index funds or ETFs, get your financial house in order.

STEP 1: Do Your Homework

There are a couple of tasks you need to do to make the right financial decisions for yourself. You can read up on these simple tasks in any self-help book on home budgeting and financial management, but here are the basics:

Take an inventory of all your assets. Assessing your earning power and taking an inventory of all your personal assets is vital when it comes to the matter of investing. You won't be able to avoid unnecessary risk if you are not sure about your own income situation and the financial reserves you have at your disposal. The old adage "nothing ventured, nothing gained" may be true, but it never implied that you should be taking dumb risks either. Get your financial house in order by measuring and assessing it. Periodically go over these numbers – perhaps once a year. It will train you to take charge of your financial affairs, which is, ultimately, the single most important step in creating an investment plan.

Check your current and potential earning power, and keep track of expenses. Equally important is the matter of saving to accumulate assets and to build a strong financial base for future investing. There is no other way around saving part of your income; accumulating cash should always be your default position. There is absolutely no pressure for you to do anything else other than accruing capital and protecting it – i.e., prevent it from decreasing – whatever an economist or financial services expert might tell you. Saving works, and it has done so across cultures and economic systems. If there is not enough money for future financial needs such as retirement, you either save more money now, work more or longer, or you create additional earnings opportunities over time so that you can save more in the future?

Once you have done your homework, you can start contemplating index fund investing in more detail, and it starts with an all-important question: how much money are you willing to lose

STEP 2: Decide Your Path

You need to be clear on what index funds are: cheap bets in the ultimate money game that is powered by Wall Street. Moreover, as we know from gambling, if you place bets, you are bound to lose a few. Hence, before you even consider joining the game, you have to checkmark the following mandatory tasks:

Study Investing

You will need to acknowledge two simple truths about investing. First, any decision involving passing on your hard-earned money to someone else contains risk, and hence, includes some elements of gambling. Second, investing is as much a subliminal decision-making process as it is a rational process. Beyond this, in purely financial terms, investing is often described as "the process of laying out money now, in the expectation of receiving more money in the future" and "the act of committing money or capital to an endeavor (a business, project, real estate, etc.) with the expectation of obtaining an additional income or profit."[128] According to this definition, there are two components to investing: capital protection and adequate returns. Basically, it says to take care of the defense first (not losing money) before you seek returns. In order to assure "safety of principle," as Benjamin Graham postulates, you need to have a mechanism to evaluate and assess each investment before a decision is made.

The main objective here is to assess the likelihood of success, i.e., return of your capital in full. Investors need to take risks to achieve returns, but to minimize the real risk of loss, its potential to generate future cash flow needs to be assessed relative to the price paid for investments now.

Understand Your Own Psychology

The bottom line is that when making decisions about money, we are constantly influenced by powerful cognitive biases. You need to be aware that with any bet that involves big money, there will be forces manipulating your decisions – from simple price manipulation through derivatives markets, flash crashes, and price moving news. There will be news in the media, and there will be plenty of experts peddling their world-view. The biggest test of them all, devastating market crashes and their economic impact, could lead to prolonged recessions and financial challenges for you. You must clearly understand the psychological impact. Hence, key questions to ask yourself include:

1. **How much are you able and willing to lose?** If the answer is "not much," then it's only prudent to make a conscious decision to stay away completely from any financial market product. Keep in mind the answer to this question is not purely mathematical – you need to understand exactly what sort of an impact losing *all* of your money will have on your life.
2. **Will you be able to psychologically withstand losses?** When you see your personal fortune down by 30% or more – what will you do? Will you be strong enough to keep on buying, even though your instincts may be telling you not to? What about the impact the views of the other people in your life?
3. **How do you react to constant exposure to financial media and expert opinions?** Do you find yourself constantly changing your investment plans? Are you easily swayed? Are you a "fiddler," following the latest fads? If you are, you'll need to work on this.

Decide If Wall Street Is For You

You must also understand that investing is not all about Wall Street, stock markets, and mutual funds, but includes a range of possible investment scenarios as diverse as the number of ETFs listed today. Academics and Wall Street folks never answered the all-important question about whether we need to be invested in stocks and mutual funds in the first place. However, once you have understood what investing really means, the real risks involved, the uncertainty of future returns, your own psychological profile, you may, in fact, decide that you would be better off staying away – and that is completely legitimate. There are two fundamental reasons why you should stay away completely:

1. You know you can't and don't want to handle the possible psychological agony and the real financial consequences related to investing in financial markets.
2. You have neither knowledge nor experience about financial market investing.

I never understood Bogle's argument that "betting is a loser's game" when selecting individual stocks or funds. According to him, "emotions are almost certain to have a powerful negative impact on the returns that investors achieve." Yet he recommends putting blind faith in the biggest bet of them all – markets always rise, and all will be fine in the long-term. However, why play Wall Street's games on their terms, and risk losing money over and over again in the process, if you could just focus on your personal earnings potential, accumulate cash, and aim to minimize the threats of inflation? Simple cash accounts and the purchase of an appropriate percentage of gold and silver will always suffice. There is absolutely no need to engage in any other games you don't understand, just because someone tries to convince you of potentially higher returns in the long-term. Those already contributing to 401(k) plans should continue to do so. Any low risk and high-quality cash solution, preferably in a low-cost form, will do.

If you do choose to invest your hard-earned cash, start with focusing on the most logical opportunities relevant to your personal circumstances. Your first investment is always in your own earnings potential. Any investment starts with an investment in yourself and your career. It could range from investing in advanced degrees or technical training to investing in your own business. All these cash layouts are investments in your future earnings potential. However, they are not risk-free – far from it – but these investments will pay out in higher income or more job variety and opportunities in which to capitalize yourself. For example, a person who studied artificial intelligence (AI) in the field of business analysis and management (particularly in the financial sector) could expect more desirable work opportunities with attractive compensation. Mark Cuban seems to agree with this trend.[129] Adding languages skills for those active in the tourist industry will most certainly increase market value. The variation and possibilities are endless, especially for those blessed to be born in industrialized countries in the West and the Far East.

Develop an Entrepreneurial Spirit

Those who have built secure income streams over the years can start working on increasing their earnings potential by either reinvesting in more of the same or considering alternative routes for diversification and wealth protection. You could consider purchasing real estate as a primary home or for income purposes. Establishing businesses is another valid alternative to increasing income and even creating earnings opportunities beyond the mandatory retirement age. There are millions of small, medium, and large enterprises that have provided valid long-term investment and income opportunities for those who created them, usually with market-beating performance. Entire family dynasties across the globe that survived over centuries have been built on this premise and a conservative diversification of their accumulated wealth, such as land and gold. Again, all this must happen in the context of paying reasonable prices for the value you receive in return.

To suggest that these forms of proactive money making efforts do not matter is ignoring the huge potential of the world's economy – and the diversity of the opportunities it offers. Why tie yourself to a bucket of stocks when you could flit around, picking and choosing the best at your own pace? Whatever your decision, it needs to be in accordance with your own psychological makeup, your greater financial circumstances, and your willingness to keep on learning and studying the subject matter in question.

STEP 3: Decide Your Strategy

If you have decided that you can handle Wall Street, financially as well as mentally – congratulations. If you're savvy, know what you're getting into, and are willing to spend time tending to your education and investments, index funds have their deserved place in the investment universe. In the hands of the informed and experienced individual, index funds can be wonderful investment tools.

I have identified two main approaches on how to make index fund investing work for you. The following two index investing approaches are neither complete nor perfect. So make sure that you have properly assessed your financial status from Step 1 before you get started. If you intend to buy index funds, this book should have already given you a good overview of what index funds and ETFs are. In the *recommended reading* section, you can continue studying index funds and the subject of investing.

The Sledgehammer Method

The first approach to index fund investing is what I like to call the *sledgehammer method*. It is the generally agreed upon investment approach to mutual fund investing: Invest on a regular basis through DCA and continue regardless of any financial collapse, crisis or financial skullduggery. I call it the sledgehammer method because it works through sheer willpower, brute force and plenty of financial resources. However, there are several caveats and adjustments I would like to clarify with this approach.

As we know, this rather direct approach hasn't worked for many retail investors in the past, so we need to discover for whom it actually did and why. If you look at Bogle's own index fund portfolio and instructions or the stereotypical successful index fund investor, we can find a few important clues. For this, we use two examples:

(1) Vanguard's counsel who helped launch the first index mutual fund in 1976 and was one of the first investors.
(2) John Bogle's own investments in index funds.

Let's look at Bogle's history of investing in his own funds. Bogle had always had a stable income through his work and other entrepreneurial activities, which came from being a renowned CEO, and later chairman, of a large financial institution. Bogle's innovative pursuits at Vanguard, especially as a spokesperson for the index fund industry, yielded him directorship positions, a respectable royalty income from speaking gigs, and book sales. I am also certain that he always had a diversified portfolio of assets that must have included some form of real estate.

The point is that he was financially well off, without much debt or overexposure to any risky assets, and he placed a heavy emphasis on regular monthly earnings streams early on in his life. According to reports, in the last ten years as head of Vanguard, Bogle received roughly $150,000 to $200,000 in annual salaries, and a similar amount in bonus payments, plus substantial payouts from Vanguard's partnership plan that gives employees a percentage of Vanguard's profits. Depending on Bogle's personal lifestyle, it's certainly not too difficult to put a portion of that total compensation aside for regular investments in index funds. Hence, successful index fund investors seem to be well off, with plenty of financial resources and an already diversified asset allocation. Therefore, they can invest in index funds as part of their wealth management strategy. Rule one of the Sledgehammer Method is to have a relatively stable monthly income. Have a diversified portfolio of income-generating assets. That could be your personal brand, your law degree, your own business, or traditional real estate for income purposes.

However, that's not all. Next, we have to assume that all winners had plenty of cash resources to continue buying, even when the average investor would naturally hesitate. This was in order to capitalize on bargain basement prices right after any financial crisis, when most people are either too frightened or simply too financially battered to make purchases. The intuitive reaction in any panic or crisis would be to stop and wait for better times, but that would automatically mean that your average purchasing price is always higher than it could be under a disciplined DCA approach. The result could be that you will always end up having much less than the indicated market returns of index funds. Thus, the second rule of the Sledgehammer Method: always have enough cash resources available to continue your base DCA, and resist the urge to stop contributing during any big market slump, i.e., have a mind of steel and overcome your own instinctive urges to stop buying (or worse, to sell). That's why you should have a stable, diversified income stream and a diversified asset portfolio in the first place.

The Sledgehammer Method was at the heart of Buffett's suggestion to LeBron James: "Buy index funds and buy them regularly, but keep substantial cash reserves."[130] James' net worth is estimated to be around $311 million. It would be an easy task for him to invest 50% in one or two broadly diversified index funds and still have plenty of cash lying around when times get rough. He can always publish his autobiography or become a consultant on all basketball-related matters – can you do that?

Ownership Society
Percent of total assets and liabilities held by wealthiest 1%, next 9% and bottom 90%

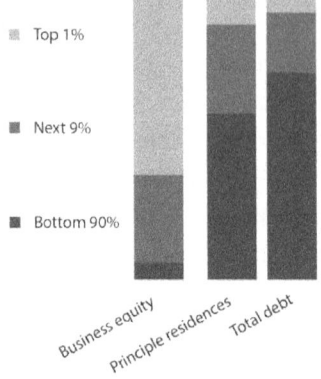

Source: Edward Wolff, New York University

Consider a more realistic case that represents a typical upper middle-class family: a $100,000 yearly budget with an (optimistic) savings rate of 15%. Let's assume that the constellation is rather stable over the next 30 years of your life, and you have already saved up $300,000 in various savings and retirement accounts with a home financed through a standard mortgage. Not a bad situation to be in. However, investing 50% of that portfolio in equities or equity index funds of any sort could be considered suicidal. In any year, you could have unbudgeted spending – home repairs, health issues, or unexpected job changes – and would have to tap into your reserves. If that happens at an inopportune moment (as it usually does), when the stock market just tanked 20% or more, you can see where this could lead to financially.

Clearly, the Sledgehammer Method doesn't work for all of us – especially with big home and consumer loans on the average American household's balance sheet. We need an alternative strategy that is simple, appropriate for our financial situation, more attuned with our inner workings and intuitive systems, and requires little input. Hence, I would like to introduce you to an alternative index investing approach, which actually can be applied to any investment class and by anyone who spends some effort to study investing and its history. It's called the opportunistic approach or, as I like to call it, the *80/20 investing approach*.

The 80/20 Approach

The Pareto's Principle, also known as the 80/20 principle, demonstrates that only a minority of causes lead to the majority of results. Everywhere in life. Studying the lives of very successful entrepreneurs and investors, only 20% or less of them generated more than 80% of their investment performance. Only a few factors contribute to extraordinary investment success. Studying these factors and focusing on these will greatly reduce your workload in the investing process and, at the same time, increase your potential performance and chances for success. Let's have a closer look at these possible factors that could lead to investing success.

The chances for a successful harvest are improved by planting seeds at the right moment; in investing, there are times to take bets, and many more times to stay away from taking any bets. It all depends on how well you understand them, your capacity for assessing the odds for each bet, and how much you are willing to pay for it. In his article "Rich Man, Poor Man," Richard Russell described it as thus:

> …When bonds are cheap and bond yields are irresistibly high, he buys bonds. When stocks are on the bargain table and stock yields are attractive, he buys stocks. When real estate is a great value, he buys real estate. When great art or fine jewelry or gold is on the "give away" table, he buys art or diamonds or gold. In other words, the wealthy investor puts his money where the great values are.[131]

In this approach, you simply make use of opportunities that financial markets offer you. There is one edge we all enjoy as individual players – the freedom to pick the time and place of our bets. In other words, we can wait for something that interests us at the right price. If nothing else is available, we have the option to say, "No, thank you," and wait. You should not take this option lightly or for granted. No institutional investors have that option; neither do full-time professional gamblers, day traders, and speculators. Professional money managers are paid to manage money, not to sit on piles of cash. If markets rise and they keep too much cash, it can seriously hurt their monthly performance. The price is of sitting on cash is the possibility of missing out – also known as "opportunity cost." For a manager, opportunity cost is a life-or-death issue. For you, it isn't.

As a result, the perfect investment vehicles for this approach are index funds and ETFs.

Let me elaborate: The opportunistic approach makes use of your cash or liquidity reserves whenever markets offer you some great opportunities in any financial asset class you feel comfortable investing in. Certainly, you can't be an expert in all of these asset classes or even a sub-section of each individual asset class. Academics are right to say that most of us pretty much stink at selecting individual securities, such as single stocks or bonds. Many of us are also not adept at selecting the right fund manager or right mutual fund. Here, all the core advantages of index funds will come to fruition. You get maximum diversification at the lowest fees possible with maximum transparency through a standard index fund managed by an institution that is most likely too big to fail. Any asset class that offers a unique investment opportunity through time can be utilized by the respective index fund or ETF. Buying a fund from one of the leading index providers will give you the additional benefit of protection through transparency and professional infrastructure. So, how do you know when to buy?

STEP 4: Execution

I have already written extensively about situations I call magic categories in my book *The 80/20 Investor*. In short, whenever there is a global financial panic, an individual country or industry panic, or even an asset class crisis, the respective index funds and ETFs can be extremely useful tools to make use of any market imbalance or panic situation that manifest itself in a crisis. Legend has it that Nathan Mayer Rothschild coined the phrase, "Buy when there's blood in the streets – even if the blood is your own."

Nowadays, we might be more familiar with the phrase, "The time to buy is when there's blood in the streets." What it means, in more abstract terms, is only buy bets that have a very high chance of a positive outcome, like those created by extreme imbalances and market situations. If the world economy takes a dive and global stocks tank by their usual 30% or more, you buy your favorite equity index funds, and keep on buying while prices continue to go down. If gold or oil crashes to historic lows, you add some index funds to your portfolio in these commodities. If the entire US real estate sector collapses, you buy high-quality real estate ETFs at bargain prices. Through this approach, the concept of "asset allocation" happens organically over time through the availability of investment opportunities, rather than through a forced theoretical concept based on multiple assumptions. I have made use of index funds on several occasions in the past, ranging from investments in particular asset classes (such as gold and oil) to specific country funds or ETFs.

Within these "magic categories," there is probably no other category where the deployment of index funds can shine more than a separate financial crisis in a single country. Through index funds, investors can get quick exposure at minimum fees, with full transparency and without the usual complications that would occur if we had to invest directly in a specific country, its currency, and its stock market. If Russia experiences a massive stock market crisis, you buy the Russian Stock Market benchmark for your portfolio. Ditto for China, for Australia, wherever.

In these situations, you will most likely be able to profit from what I like to call a *double discount* phenomenon. You could profit not only from much lower market prices caused by a selling panic, but also from a weakened local currency, which usually accompanies any financial crisis as a sign of loss of confidence in that particular country. If you look at any of the individual country crises in the past 100 years, you will recognize the same pattern over and over again. And contrary to what you may think, if it happened in your own country, your opportunities may be even better. You can act on what I like to call a citizen *lender of the last resort*.[132] This can only be possible if you haven't contributed in any buying frenzy or bubble situation in the first place. If you keep calm and resist urges to join the herd, you will have plenty of cash resources available when the occasional financial crisis occurs, and they always do. And these crises don't only apply to world economies, but industries, individual companies and asset classes.

Then there is the question of how much you buy in each opportunity. The answer to that depends on your personal assessment from *Step 1*, and the country or asset class in question. If you already have a diversified portfolio of assets and a stable monthly income with plenty of cash reserves, I don't see any harm in deploying a good portion of that accumulated cash – that's what we have been saving for in the first place. Depending on how convinced you are about each investment opportunity, you could even sell existing investments in your portfolio. Personally, I never follow a rigid top-down asset allocation approach based on arbitrary forecasts, nor do I divide my portfolio into slices that have to fit a whimsical asset allocation model that looks good on paper. What always helped were plenty of cash reserves and a stable monthly income. Regular portfolio adjustments and reshuffling to cash is just part of a very natural process that depends on the opportunities available.

Nikkei 225 – Japan's Hidden Opportunities

If you use an opportunistic approach to investing, you will do less trading, be less bothered with market volatility, and most likely achieve better annualized returns than a mindless DCA plan. Let me give you an illustration of how this approach can work in even the most challenging market environments. Consider the case of Japan's stock market by utilizing a Japanese index fund or ETF.

The Japanese stock market has been a graveyard for many institutional and retail investors alike. Local Japanese investors would send you packing if you recommended a traditional DCA plan for their home equities market. This is one of the reasons why the central bank of Japan (BOJ) has been desperately trying to prop the local stock market up with its own ETF purchasing program. The BOJ is, in all probability, the largest shareholder of all Japanese stocks as of December 2016.

However, that doesn't mean that it hasn't offered 80/20 investors many opportunities to make a killing in Japanese stocks with the help of simple index funds or ETFs. In late 2002, the Japanese banking sector was on the brink of total disaster – certainly by November 2002, you could see that something was very wrong. One headline from the *International Herald Tribune* on November 16th/17th 2002 read "Japan combats banking fears – Nationalization talk hits stock." Shares of UFJ (the fourth largest lender) in Japan fell by 19% in two days. Concurrently, the Nikkei 225 dropped quickly from 12,000 to almost 7,800, a 25-year low, and an 80% drop from its historic peak of 38,900 in 1989.

Now, let's assume you bought a Japanese index fund or ETF at levels below 10,000. Over the course of days and weeks, you added to the position at lower prices until you had invested 10% or even 15% of your investment portfolio – all out of your cash and liquidity reserves. With this bet, you would have speculated on the recovery of the world's second-largest economy, and a consequential recovery of its stock market (without knowing much about each stock within the index). At the beginning of 2007, the Nikkei 225 would trade at 17,000, offering a capital gain of roughly 100% for a 4-year holding period that included a 2% annual dividend yield – roughly a 20% annualized return.

At this point, a conservative investor familiar with Japan and Japan's economy would have sold the index funds with gusto. They would have known that the index could not maintain such high annual rates going forward, due to its future economic and demographic outlook.

Now, let's assume that you sold your entire Nikkei 225 position, and then re-entered the market during the subprime crises that originated with the bankruptcy of Lehman Brothers. The Nikkei 225 would trade at new lows of 7,200 – definitely a shock for most investors, but not for 80/20 investors. At this point, you would have added more, doubling or even tripling your initial investment at much lower prices (at a time when Japan's finest companies traded near liquidation value, as if they weren't operating at all). This time it wasn't a homemade problem, but a problem that originated in the US financial sector. As a matter of fact, the Japanese financial sector would prove to be the most sound in the industrial world, even bailing out Morgan Stanley and Goldman Sachs with fresh capital investments at the height of the crisis. Today, at the beginning of 2017, the Nikkei trades at around 20,000.

Keep in mind that not every asset or country crisis works out with a happy ending – Greece and Venezuela are prime examples that would tax the patience of even the most long-term-oriented investor. This approach is not risk-free and requires you to study the asset class in question, but it does give you a wide area of possible investment opportunities to look for. While this distinct approach might not be suitable for every retail investor, particularly those who prefer minimum activity, more experienced investors with cash reserves and stable incomes should consider it. It's not often that markets offer you oil at $27 a barrel or gold at less than $300 or even Asian stocks or Latin American stocks at bargain basement prices and very favorable exchange rates.

There is another advantage of this approach – inactivity pays. Let's assume, you see an opportunity, such as crude oil, trading at the ridiculously low price of $27 a barrel or less (as it did in 2016), but you feel uninformed or just uncomfortable buying a Vanguard or BlackRock oil ETF. You let it pass, and that is fine. No harm done. You aren't competing with your neighbor, co-worker, or professional money manager for outperformance. It isn't your job to maximize potential profit opportunities with more risk than you can handle. Your main job is to secure your capital and improve the odds of success for any investment decision you might be considering. That's the power we, as individual investors have – to let it pass.

When to Sell

If you had been so fortuitous to buy at bargain basement prices, you are in a very strong position with plenty of options. You could just hold and keep your position forever. Alternatively, you could sell all or parts, at handsome profits. For example, if you bought a Nikkei 225 ETF at an average price of 8,000, you are in a very comfortable position, regardless of the economic outlook forecast by economists and financial market experts. The same counts for holders of S&P 500 index funds and ETFs who bought between 2008 and 2009 at an average price of 900 to 1,000. You could hold on to your positions indefinitely. However, there are some convincing arguments why you should consider selling parts of your position or even your complete position.

Consider the following arguments: The average expected return for US index funds is projected to be between 7% to 8%. Thanks to your clever buying at the very end of the subprime crisis, you can record an annualized return of 20% or more for holding your index fund position for roughly six years. It's time to take profits. The reason is simple. In the long-term, you wouldn't be able to maintain these very high annualized returns, as they would revert back to the mean of 7% to 8% (or most likely much lower) returns going forward. In short, your average returns can only go down from here while exposing yourself to the regular market madness and exuberance. For example, your index funds could be flat for several years or even go down over time entering a new bear market. Your annualized returns must necessarily decrease to historic averages the longer you keep them – that's called mean reversion. This is the same phenomenon Bogle has been writing about, but from the opposite direction.

This goes hand in hand with the next argument. Selling all or parts of your holdings would give you ample amounts of cash and liquid reserves for the next financial crisis or market folly down the road. Remember the *optionality of cash* is always a valuable option to have. You will have plenty of firepower to make use of any new opportunity markets periodically offer you. Also, you might sleep better with plenty of money at your side. In the case of Nikkei or US ETFs today, it would certainly be a valid option to cash in all or some of the gains from previous years.

Finally, keep in mind that, thanks to globalized financial markets and electronic trading, financial markets today are inherently different from the past. They should have become more rational and less volatile, thanks to the efficient distribution of market news and more sophisticated market players. As we all know, this is just an idealized fantasy. Flash crashes and price exuberances are very much a part of daily financial markets today, as are the human fallacies of which we are all aware. Global financial markets seem to have become more erratic and volatile, because every bit of change could be a potential play for leveraged gains or losses. Charlie Munger, vice chairman of Berkshire Hathaway, had this to say about the current state of financial markets: "A vast gambling culture, and people have made it respectable." Most of the time, it's just better to stay away from it all by taking the chips off the table and going home, rather than to be a constant part of extreme market folly.

Final Verdict

I have always asked myself why the opportunistic approach to investing is not more common, as it has some obvious advantages for individual investors. One reason, perhaps, is that this approach is extremely disadvantageous to the financial industry, as well to academic analysts. Due to the fact that by definition, an opportunistic approach is sporadic, this approach is difficult to measure or put into a rigorous academic framework. Furthermore, no business on this planet could survive on a business model that relies on the randomness and fickleness of its consumers. No index fund provider or Wall Street institution has ever been interested in reducing the inflow of money by recommending staying away or reducing financial market investments. If all the brokers on this planet had customers who traded once or twice a year and kept their wallet closed the rest of the time, most of them would be out of business within a year or less.

Nevertheless, the opportunistic approach has stood the test of time. In a sense, it embodies the way most of us do our daily and seasonal shopping. If you need to buy milk, you buy it when you need it, and you make sure you get value for the price you pay. On days you don't need milk, you don't buy it – as simple as that. You don't buy most of your food on a subscription basis either. If prices are ridiculously high, you would stay away completely and go for cheaper alternatives. However, when prices drop, you would most likely continue buying, maybe even a bit more than usual if something is on sale (like the infamous "buy one get one free"). The point is, you wouldn't stop buying out of fear that it could drop even further. Warren Buffett explained:

> "If you're buying groceries, you like it when prices go down next week. And you like it if they go down further the next week. Just as we like getting a good deal on the items at the grocery store we

would be buying anyway, we should also be fans of getting a good deal on our favorite companies."[133]

The analogy of grocery shopping was first made famous by Benjamin Graham, professor and mentor to Warren Buffett. He notes:

> "If you are shopping for common stocks, choose them the way you would buy groceries, not the way you would buy perfume."[134]

The whole message of his analogy is that you need to think for yourself whenever you make a purchasing decision; you just can't switch off your brain in the hope something good will come out of it. But here comes the decisive difference between grocery shopping and the purchase of stocks, index funds, and all sorts of esoteric financial products that can be bought today. Do we really need to buy them, like we do our grocery shopping? Do we need to invest in stocks? Do we really need financial markets, Wall Street and their sales and advisory armies to survive? Low interest rates are just not an excuse for the financial risks you are taking to acclaim it as a life necessity.

This question often results in a heated debate among professionals, academia, and the media. My point is that no doubt, we should always be investing in something relevant to us. But does it have to be on Wall Street? Do we really need the latest ETF and to trade it all day long – maybe on some fancy new indices and asset classes, or maybe even with substantial financial leverage? My belief is that we don't, because we all have the investment opportunities right at our fingertips: education, training, experience, property, land, and even our own businesses.

Seeing it from this perspective would give us enormous power over any salesperson who has something to sell to us. We don't need Wall Street – we don't need stocks or mutual funds and index funds – so we can say no at any time. If another financial

Armageddon happens, as it surely will, we will readily have the financial reserves and become the "citizen lender of the last resort." We might even do our country a real service in showing trust and confidence when it needed it the most. With that spirit, we could weather even the largest financial tsunami.

When it comes to index funds, therefore, I would call them a useful tool in the wide arsenal of investment tools that we, as self-responsible citizens, have at our disposal to achieve our financial goals. At the moment, there is no bigger herd than the collective group of growing index fund investors, and my most concise advice is this: don't be one of them. In famed portfolio manager Jeremy Grantham's view, "This herd-like behavior is the primary reason securities markets are incredibly inefficient and present opportunities for the true contrarian investor."[135]

Not thinking for yourself, resting on your own passivity, and blindly following an industry that has proven over and over again that its own self-interest is paramount can never be the answer. The only realistic solution is self-responsibility.

Whenever academics, especially in the field of economics, suggest a new revolutionary investment approach based on their elaborate theories and assumptions, you should listen attentively, but leave your wallet perfectly zipped. Rather than supplying fees and handing over your precious "capital" on a silver platter, you will be able to execute your own "unconventional" investment strategy, and in the process, be able to protect your savings and earn adequate returns.

My vision and hope are to see the number of independently-thinking investors increase among the masses of lost retail investors. I truly hope that more and more individuals will be able to resist and escape the grasp of more experienced players and aggressive sales promoters. When this happens, we will be much closer to Bogle's vision of true owners' capitalism.

DAVID SCHNEIDER

Afterword

John C. Bogle deserves the respect he has received over his long career. He has always believed that long-term buy-and-hold investing in stock markets is the best strategy for the common man, and that one simple benchmark index fund is the best vehicle for that strategy. He created a financial product based on sound and logical thinking, backed up by academic research, in order to provide an efficient investment product and circumvent the enduring flaws of professional money management. He was the original "disruptor" of the mutual fund world, and he changed its status quo. He brought extreme imbalances to the once so profitable world of money management, and to his credit was called many names by his peers throughout his career.

However, over the decades, and with increased momentum in recent years, the concept of index investing has been exploited by their providers. Even Bogle must admit that index funds and their providers have been moving in a direction that doesn't seem to resemble the initial spirit of his innovation. For his criticism and warnings, he was publicly ridiculed as a doddering old fool – ironically, by the people who should be most grateful to Bogle for helping them create a trillion-dollar business in the first place.

Bogle is not alone in his criticism. Ironically, BlackRock CEO Larry Fink, speaking at an industry conference in 2014, warned that structural problems with leveraged ETFs have the potential to "blow up the whole industry one day."[136] Even more perplexing, only a year later, famed investor Carl Icahn (good friend and private advisor to President Donald Trump) openly criticized BlackRock for misleading individual investors into very risky ETFs. At an investor's conference, while sitting next to Fink, he claimed that: "They [BlackRock] are putting their name on this stuff and people are buying it. …..BlackRock is an extremely dangerous company."[137] Icahn accused the giant money management firm of contributing to various asset class bubbles by diverting individual investors into its funds and ETFs that are far from being safe and prudent investments. At one point in the heated discussion, Icahn compared BlackRock with banks in the 2007 subprime crisis, when they sold billions of dollars of faulty subprime mortgage bonds.[138] With $5 trillion in assets under their direct reign, and probably commanding much more than that, BlackRock is certainly a case of "too big to fail" that the taxpayer will have to sort out in any worst case scenario. It would certainly be a "cruel irony" if the same industry that intended to protect and insulate the little guy from abusive Wall Street practices blows up.

Bogle could sit back, relax and enjoy his retirement in peace, rather than risk being ridiculed by his former peers and competitors. As of 2014, he made a fortune estimated at $88 million. Bogle got independently wealthy, not off index funds but as an entrepreneurial investor who took calculated risks for his wealth and his career. The income he earned from these personal investments powered all his future asset purchases, including his regular contributions to index funds. In short, even the godfather of index funds made most of his money outside of actually investing in index funds.

In an article that appeared in the Boston Globe in 2006, Bogle shared his compensation package for his final years at Vanguard: "He was paid roughly $200,000 in salary and a $300,000 bonus in 1991, plus around $2 million under a partnership plan that gave employees a percentage of Vanguard's profits." Critics saw this as evidence that "the Partnership Plan has proven more profitable to

Vanguard executives than Vanguard's funds have been to shareholders." Yet his successors and his peers have extracted far more from the industry – indicative of how their relationships with their investors have changed. He never really profited from the "index fund revolution" the same way his peers did. It is the current and next generation of Vanguard's top managers and executives who will reap all the financial rewards of the secretive partnership plan.

Bogle was never exploitative or overly demanding when it came to benefits and compensation plans, even though he was entitled to much more. In the early 1990s, he even gave back about 40% of his partnership share to Vanguard. His reasoning: He didn't want to be greedy, something you won't hear very often within the financial industry. Among his avid followers and within the mutual fund industry, Bogle turned into a legend, a strange figure who refused to take his entire compensation because he felt obliged to his shareholders and his many loyal clients. When Bogle resigned (i.e., was forced to resign) as Chairman in 1999, the money management industry lost its original disruptor and most fervent critic. You could hear sighs of relief among the remaining captains as their universe was finally restored, and the waters offered clear sailing ahead on a course only too familiar. In the end, it was always, "Stay the course."

Would You Like to Know More?

I am aware, that I can't change a person's habits with a single book. Hence, to encourage positive action through continuous learning and training, I provide a range of free investing resources.

I am the host of the 80/20 Investing Show, a podcast and YouTube channel where I regularly publish posts on financial markets, investing research and education. Visit www.8020investors.com to get more information and access to all my free resources:

Thank You

Before you go, I'd like to say "thank you" for purchasing this book. These days, we are flooded with free content and investment guides that promise the world. So, a big thanks for downloading this book and reading all the way to the end. In the words of my self-publishing hero Steve Scott: "If you liked what you've read then I need your help. Please take a moment to leave a review for this book on Amazon." Let others know that this book has quality and value for readers interested in this subject. — Thank you.

Acknowledgements

I would like to thank my launch team and all the people who reviewed and critiqued this book. Special thanks to my editorial team. My editor, Subodhana Wijeyeratne, has been a great help in formulating some general arguments on a complex topic – and undoubtedly has put his stamp on this piece of work. His wealth of historical knowledge has been extremely helpful in identifying some of the trends discussed here. I would also be remiss in not mentioning the tireless efforts of Valerie Smith, as critical voice and eye of the team. Both are very talented writers, whom I highly recommend. I am grateful to my production team, which encompasses designers, a narrator, proofreaders, and many more. I would like to thank my numerous friends from the DC community, my mastermind groups, as well as my sources and contacts in the financial industry who have always offered a helping hand and their personal views. As always, I am grateful to my parents. They gave me all the opportunities a son could wish for, which has allowed me to explore the world.

Recommended Reading

On Index Funds

Birdthistle, William A.. **Empire of the Fund**: The Way We Save Now. Oxford University Press. Kindle Edition. One of the best books on mutual funds. A very technical book about mutual fund with a rigorous, thorough and critical analysis for the world of mutual funds and its providers.

Bogle, John. **Little Book Of Common Sense Investing**. Wiley. 2007. The ultimate bible on index funds and index investing. If you want to know what the founder of Vanguard and the first retail index mutual fund thinks about the true nature of index investing and the state of the industry, you have to read this book.

Braham, Lewis. **The House that Bogle Built:** How John Bogle and Vanguard Reinvented the Mutual Fund Industry. McGraw-Hill Education; 1 edition (April 18, 2011). An excellent account about Vanguard's journey to the top and the maker behind it. Behind the doors operations, politics and sales strategies. Many times, reads like a corporate thriller.

Ferri, Richard A.. **The Power of Passive Investing**. John Wiley & Sons. Kindle Edition. One of the best books on index funds. More technical and detailed, but gives a good overview of all the academic arguments in the index fund and efficient market discussion. Also, it provides a technical discussion on how financial advisors should approach the topic of index funds and passive investing.

On Investing

Graham, Benjamin (2006). ***The Intelligent Investor***: the definitive book on value investing. New York, NY: HarperCollins Publishing, Inc., It's the bible of value investing and the according to Warren Buffett the best book ever written on the subject of investing. Particularly chapter 8 and 20 are important to read several times over.

Buffett, Warren. ***Buffett's Shareholders Letters of Berkshire Hathaway.*** Warren Buffett might be a proponent of index fund investing for the common man, but all his letters (particularly the earlier ones) tell a different story. It's a story about beating markets by investing unconventionally and rigorously demanding value for the price paid. A real education on the topic of intelligent investing.

Poor Charlie's Almanack: The Wit and Wisdom of Charles T. Munger. Donning Co Pub; 2nd Expanded edition . 2005. Gives an excellent introduction to the world of behavioral economics and a great summary of human misjudgment and cognitive biases.

GLOSSARY

Assets Under Management (AUM): Is the total market value of assets that an investment company or financial institution manages on behalf of investors.

Black Swan Event: An event that comes as a surprise, has a major effect, and is often inappropriately rationalized after the fact with the benefit of hindsight. Nassim Taleb who popularized the term regards almost all major scientific discoveries, historical events, and artistic accomplishments as "black swans" – undirected and unpredicted. He gives the rise of the Internet, the personal computer, World War I, dissolution of the Soviet Union, and the September 2001 attacks as examples of black swan events.

Cash Engine: An engine that produces cash non-stop as long as it runs. Anybody can earn money, and if you end up spending less than you make, you have a positive cash flow. You are yourself your primary cash engine—take good care of it.

Flash Crash: The quick drop and recovery in securities prices usually caused by computer glitches, flawed programming or order manipulation.

Financial Leverage: Refers to the use of debt to acquire additional assets. A lot of traders borrow money to magnify small speculation gains.

Fund of Funds (FOF): Funds that invest in other funds managed by other companies or different fund managers. It not only spreads the risk of each diversified fund but also among different fund strategies or asset classes. Of course, all this risk diversification comes at a price in the form of another layer of management fees for the managers of the Fund of Funds.

Investor's Itch: An investor's psychological weakness to have the urge to be active, because they think they might lose out or miss some exciting action.

Magic Categories: Areas 80/20 investors prefer to search for investment opportunities, in order to reduce the workload and achieve above average returns.

Market Capitalization: Is the market value of a listed company derived from multiplying its total number of shares outstanding with the current market price.

Optionality of Cash: Is a permanent option that holder's of cash possess, to either keep cash or to invests it in any asset class, within any industry at any time of the holder's liking and personal preference. Institutional investors including most hedge funds and private equity funds don't have that option.

Overpayment Risk: The most important risk definition for retail investors. It is the risk of paying too much for an investment target than the real value you receive in return. Overpayment usually leads to deferred losses.

Quant Hedge Funds: A sophisticated and complex hedge fund trading strategy using quantitative analysis and computer-based models in order to calculate the mathematical odds of each bet versus the invested capital necessary, while aiming to reduce the statistical form of risk.

Tail risk: A rare form of portfolio risk that—"The possibility that an investment will move more than three standard deviations from the mean is greater than what is shown by a normal distribution."

Ultra High Net Worth Individuals (UHNWI): A person with investable assets of at least US$30 million, excluding personal assets and property such as one's primary residence, collectibles, and consumer durables. UHNWIs comprise the richest people in the world and control a disproportionate amount of global wealth.

About the Author

DAVID SCHNEIDER is the author of the bestselling The 80/20 Investor. He bought his first stock in 1994 at age 18. Subsequently, he trained as a commercial banker, research analyst and investment manager. He developed a bottom-up value approach for selecting investment opportunities and managing concentrated portfolios based on the 80/20 principle. Since 2011 David has been an independent investor, researcher, and writer. On his research blog and financial podcast—8020investors.com he covers topics including wealth management, financial markets and investment opportunities around the world.

Get in Touch:

Twitter
https://twitter.com/WooSchneider

LinkedIn
https://jp.linkedin.com/in/WooSchneider

E-mail
info@thewritingale.com

More from the Author:

The 80/20 Investor: Investing in an Uncertain and Complex World

"Are you ready to set yourself free?" The 80/20 Investor, harnessing the power of the 80/20 principle, simplifies investing. In no time, you will learn where to look for "no-brainer" opportunities, find out how to finance your investment opportunities and minimize risks. This book allows you enter the seemingly intimidating world of investing, with valuable tips from some of those who have changed the game – the Rothschilds, Hetty Green, J. Paul Getty, Henry Singleton, and others. Only with financial freedom can you live the life you want to lead. Let The 80/20 Investor show you the way.

Modern Investing: Gambling in Disguise

Modern Investing is an indispensable guide to becoming an independent investor, rather than giving in to forces that regularly turn us into gamblers or speculators. It will cover the basics every investor needs to know to start a successful investment career free of manipulation and dependence on "experts." By understanding investment history and its core principles, and contrasting it to the gambling culture of today, predominant financial scams and the peculiarities of our financial-political complex, you will be able to draw your own conclusions. More importantly, you will realize what options you still possess to make logical and independent decisions.

With the knowledge garnered from this book, you will be able to avoid scams and Wall Street chicanery; and most importantly, you will be able to establish a base investment strategy that can outperform any professional money manager, without the conventional risks. Buy this book and become an independent investor.

NOTES

[1] DALBAR. Dalbar's annual Quantitative Analysis Of Investor Behavior, 2014
[2] A significant part of this increase is due to rising stock prices since 2010
[3] Birdthistle, William A. *Empire of the Fund: The Way We Save Now.* Oxford University Press. Kindle Edition. 2016
[4] Ferri, Richard A. *The Power of Passive Investing.* John Wiley & Sons. Kindle Edition. 2010
[5] ETF insight. "Index Providers." Accessed February 28, 2017. http://www.etfinsight.ca/?page_id=15043
[6] IFIC. "The History of Mutual Funds." Accessed February 28, 2017. https://www.ific.ca/en/articles/who-we-are-history-of-mutual-funds/The History of Mutual Funds
[7] Galbraith, Kenneth. *The Great Crash of 1929: An International Disaster of Perverse Economic Policies.* (New York: Mariner Books, 2009)
[8] Cohan, William D. *Money and Power: How Goldman Sachs Came to Rule the World.* (New York: Knopf Doubleday, 2011)
[9] Galbraith, p. 26
[10] Galbraith.
[11] EH.net. "The 1929 Stock Market Crash." Accessed February 28, 2017. http://eh.net/encyclopedia/the-1929-stock-market-crash/
[12] Galbraith, Kenneth, p. 154
[13] This piece of legislation was only overturned in the late 1990s.
[14] IFIC. "The History of Mutual Funds." Accessed February 28, 2017. https://www.ific.ca/en/articles/who-we-are-history-of-mutual-funds/The History of Mutual Funds
[15] Brooks, John. *The Go-Go Years: The Drama and Crashing Finale of Wall Street's Bullish 60s.* (Hoboken: John Wiley & Sons 1999), p.131
[16] Cohan
[17] Ferri, Richard A. *The Power of Passive Investing.* (Hoboken: John Wiley &

Sons, 2010), p. 19
[18] Ferri.
[19] IFIC. "The History of Mutual Funds." Accessed February 28, 2017. https://www.ific.ca/en/articles/who-we-are-history-of-mutual-funds/The History of Mutual Funds
[20] Brooks, p. 131
[21] Brooks.
[22] Brooks.
[23] Federal Reserve fund rates averaged 11.2% in 1979, reaching a peak of 20% in June 1981 under Paul Volcker – an unthinkable figure today.
[24] James Simmons from Renaissance Technologies LLC, and Edward O. Thorp, founder of Newport Partners and Edward O. Thorp & Associates, are prime examples of academics entering the business of active money management.
[25] According to Vanguard, as of June 30, 2016, they manage more than $3.5 trillion in global assets,
[26] Statista. "Statistics and facts on mutual funds." https://www.statista.com/topics/1441/mutual-funds/ (Accessed February 28, 2017.
[27] Zweig, Jason. "Are Index Funds Eating the World?" http://jasonzweig.com/are-index-funds-eating-the-world (Accessed February 28, 2017)
[28] The cost for traditional mutual funds and index funds alike are measured as *expense ratios*, which is simply a ratio of the fund's *total operating expenses* divided by the average dollar value of its *assets under management* (AUM).
[29] Robbins, Tony. *MONEY Master the Game: 7 Simple Steps to Financial Freedom*. (New York: Simon and Schuster, 2014)
[30] Bogle, John. *Little Book Of Common Sense Investing*. (Hoboken: Wiley, 2007). p.16
[31] Financial Times. "86% of active equity funds underperform." https://www.ft.com/content/e555d83a-ed28-11e5-888e-2eadd5fbc4a4. (Accessed February 28, 2017)
[32] Bogle.
[33] ICI Global. "Frequently Asked Questions About the U.S. ETF Market." https://www.ici.org/etf_resources/background/faqs_etfs_market

(Accessed February 28, 2017)
[34] This figure includes non-index ETFs
[35] ETFdb.com. "Largest ETFs: Top 100 ETFs By Assets." http://etfdb.com/compare/market-cap/. (Accessed February 28, 2017)
[36] US Debt Clock. Accessed February 28, 2017. http://www.usdebtclock.org/
[37] Birdthistle, William A. *Empire of the Fund: The Way We Save Now.* (Oxford: Oxford University Press, 2016.)
[38] Bogle.
[39] Investopedia. "What is 'Tail Risk'." http://www.investopedia.com/terms/t/tailrisk.asp (Accessed February 28, 2017).
[40] Robbins.
[41] Bogle, p. 23
[42] Bogle
[43] Bogle
[44] Hazlitt, Henry. "Economics in One Lesson: The Shortest & Surest Way to Understand Basic Economics"
[45] Orrell, David. *Economyths: Ten Ways Economics Get It Wrong.* (Hoboken: Wiley, 2010) p. 123
[46] Richard H. Thaler. *Misbehaving: The Making of Behavioral Economics* (New York: W. W. Norton & Company, 2016), Kindle locations 1632-1633.
[47] Investopedia. "Equity Risk Premium.". http://www.investopedia.com/terms/e/equityriskpremium.asp (Accessed February 28, 2017)

[48] To calculate the equity-risk premium, subtract the risk free rate from the return of a stock over a period of time. For example, if the return on a stock is 17%, and the risk-free rate over the same period of time is 9%, then the equity-risk premium would be 8% for the stock over that period of time.
[49] You can read and study how mutual fund providers describe risk from any standard *offering memorandum* under the section titled "Risk Factors."
[50] Huang, Nellie S.. "The Hidden Dangers of Index Funds." http://www.kiplinger.com/article/investing/T030-C009-S003-the-hidden-dangers-of-index-funds.html (Accessed February 28, 2017)

[51] Greenblatt, Joel. *The Big Secret for the Small Investor: A New Route to Long-Term Investment Success.* (New York: Simon & Schuster. 2011)
[52] Arnott, Robert. Financial Analyst Journal, March/April 2005 edition,
[53] ETF.com. "Bogle and Malkiel Fight Back." http://www.etf.com/publications/journalofindices/joi-articles/2328.html?nopaging=1. (Accessed February 28, 2017)
[54] "John Bogle and Burton Malkiel Riding an Aging Bull." *Wall Street Journal*, June 27, 2006.
[55] Barron's. "Riding an Aging Bull." 2017.http://www.barrons.com/articles/SB50001424053111190369780457 6427964181984714 (Accessed February 28)
[56] Zweig, Jason. "Are Index Funds Eating the World?" http://jasonzweig.com/are-index-funds-eating-the-world/ (Accessed February 28, 2017)
[57] Zweig
[58] Alster, Norm. "The Ease of Index Funds Comes With Risk" https://www.nytimes.com/2015/10/11/business/mutfund/the-ease-of-index-funds-comes-with-risk.html?_r=0 (Accessed February 28, 2017)
[59] Alster
[60] Fraser-Jenkins, Inigo. "The Silent Road to Serfdom: Why Passive Investing is Worse Than Marxism." (New York: Sanford C. Bernstein & Co. 2016)
[61] BESPOKE. "Historical S&P 500 Sector Weightings.". https://www.bespokepremium.com/think-big-blog/historical-sp-500-sector-weightings/t (Accessed February 28, 2017)
[62] Bloomberg. "Vanguard's Gerry O'Reilly Offers a Rare Look Inside an Index Fund. https://www.bloomberg.com/news/articles/2016-08-15/vanguard-s-gerry-o-reilly-offers-a-rare-look-inside-an-index-fund. (Accessed February 28, 2017)
[63] Moral hazard is defined as "lack of incentive to guard against risk when one is protected from its consequences"
[64] Zweig.
[65] Jones, Harvey. 'Burst of the Bond Bubble could leave Biggest Mess of All'. http://www.thenational.ae/business/personal-finance/burst-of-the-bond-bubble-could-leave-the-biggest-mess-of-all (Accessed 5th March 2017)

[66] Charlie Munger, **Daily Journal** meeting March 2015
[67] CNN Money. "A Billionaire's Warning on Index Funds." http://money.cnn.com/2015/03/31/investing/investing-index-funds-warning/. (Accessed February 28, 2017)
[68] Zweig.
[69] BusinessInsider. "Here is the letter the world's largest investor, BlackRock CEO Larry Fink, just sent to CEOs everywhere." http://www.businessinsider.com/blackrock-ceo-larry-fink-letter-to-ceos-2017-1. (Accessed February 28, 2017)
[70] "Tropical MBA Episode 332." https://docs.google.com/document/d/1WKmgXrBGhYtBo0INJ_83DymvzQxDE2ZAjauFk_KDLeM/edit. (Accessed February 28, 2017)
[71] "Stocks — Part XXX: jlcollinsnh vs. Vanguard." http://jlcollinsnh.com/2016/09/15/stocks-part-xxx-jlcollinsnh-vs-vanguard/. (Accessed February 28, 2017)
[72] STATISTA. "Number of Exchange-Traded Funds (ETFs) worldwide from 2003 to 2015." https://www.statista.com/statistics/278249/global-number-of-etfs/. (Accessed February 28, 2017)
[73] Investopedia. "5 Things You Need To Know About Index Funds." http://www.investopedia.com/articles/investing/103114/5-things-you-need-know-about-index-funds.asp. (Accessed February 28, 2017)
[74] Robbins.
[75] InvestmentNews. "BlackRock fights lawsuit claiming 'excessive fees'." http://www.investmentnews.com/article/20140814/FREE/140819950/blackrock-fights-lawsuit-claiming-excessive-fees. (Accessed February 28, 2017)
[76] *Ibid.*
[77] Robbins.
[78] "A fake Rolex will never be a Rolex." Robbins.
[79] The team at Stronghold (www.strongholdfinancial.com) currently uses the All Weather portfolio as one of the many options available to their clients.
[80] MarketWatch. "Tony Robbins doesn't quite master the game of money in his new book." http://www.marketwatch.com/story/tony-robbins-doesnt-quite-master-the-game-of-money-in-his-new-book-2014-11-25. (Accessed February 28, 2017)

[81] The technical term for this scenario is called "breaking the buck"
[82] Birdthistle.
[83] *Ibid.*
[84] New York Times. "In Target-Date Funds, Hidden Homework." http://www.nytimes.com/2009/10/15/your-money/15TARGET.html. (Accessed February 28, 2017.)
[85] Ferri
[86] Brokenleginvesting.com. "Why Index Investing Will Lead To Poverty In Retirement." http://brokenleginvesting.com/2016/09/11/passive-index-investing-poverty-in-retirement/ (Accessed February 28, 2017.)
[87] MarketWatch. "7 reasons why retirement savers fail" http://www.marketwatch.com/story/7-reasons-why-retirement-savers-fail-2013-06-26. (Accessed February 28, 2017)
[88] Robbins.
[89] Bloomberg. "Index Funds, Quants and Hedging."

https://www.bloomberg.com/view/articles/2016-11-28/index-funds-quants-and-hedging (Accessed February 28, 2017)

[90] Birdthistle.
[91] Bogle.
[92] Ellis, Charles D.. *The Index Revolution: Why Investors Should Join It Now.* (Hoboken: Wiley, 2016)
[93] BBC. "How do we really make decisions?". http://www.bbc.com/news/science-environment-26258662 (Accessed February 28, 2017)
[94] *Ibid.*
[95] Thaler.
[96] GALLUP. "Gallup's annual Economy and Finance survey." http://www.gallup.com/poll/182816/little-change-percentage-americans-invested-market.aspx (Accessed February 28, 2017)
[97] Morningstar.com. "Indexing, Vanguard Drove Global Fund Flows." http://sg.morningstar.com/ap/news/Market-Watch/156406/Indexing,-Vanguard-Drove-2016-Global-Fund-Flows.aspx. (Accessed February 28, 2017)
[98] Yahoo Finance. "Analyst sounds the alarm on the 'most crowded trade

in investing history." http://finance.yahoo.com/news/analyst-sounds-the-alarm-on-the-most-crowded-trade-in-investing-history-180954941.html. (Accessed February 28, 2017)

[99] Braham, Lewis. *The House that Bogle Built: How John Bogle and Vanguard Reinvented the Mutual Fund Industry.* (New York: McGraw-Hill Education, 2011)

[100] Buffet, Warren. Berkshire Hathaway Shareholder Letter, 2003.

[101] CNBC Squawk Box, March 2nd 2015

[102] Hebner, Mark T.. *Index Funds: The 12-Step Recovery Program for Active Investors.* (New Delhi: IFA Publications, 2012)

[103] Robbins

[104] *Ibid.*

[105] Robbins.

[106] Bogle, p.71

[107] "The Expected S&P 500 Returns 2015-2025." http://theconservativeincomeinvestor.com/2015/08/13/the-expected-sp-500-returns-2015-2025/. (Accessed February 28, 2017)

[108] Hebner.

[109] Bogle, p.32

[110] Robbins.

[111] NerdWallet. "2016 American Household Credit Card Debt Study." https://www.nerdwallet.com/blog/average-credit-card-debt-household/ (Accessed February 28, 2017)

[112] "BlackRock executive Charles Hallac, dies at 50." http://www.reuters.com/article/us-blackrock-copresident-idUSKCN0R92J320150909#4TSASgekEB6rCw3G.97. (Accessed February 28, 2017)

[113] The TSP is the retirement plan that the federal government offers to its employees, and it resembles a very simple 401(k).

[114] "BlackRock SuperPacs." https://www.opensecrets.org/pacs/lookup2.php?cycle=2016&strID=C00479246. (Accessed February 28, 2017)

[115] "Vanguard Reports First Wave Of 2016 Expense Ratio Changes." https://pressroom.vanguard.com/news/Press-release-VG-announces-first-wave-expense-ratio-changes-12-22-16.html. (Accessed February 28, 2017)

[116] Braham.
[117] Financial Times. "Father of passives has doubts about ETFs." https://www.ft.com/content/1cd71934-c716-11e4-8e1f-00144feab7de. (Accessed February 28, 2017)
[118] Manson, Mark. "How Your Insecurity Is Bought and Sold." https://markmanson.net/insecurity (Accessed February 28, 2017)
[119] Ferri.
[120] See Senate Report, 1970, U.S.C.C.A.N., 4897, 4907, interpreted by the 2nd Circuit Court of Appeals in Gartenberg v. Merrill Lynch Asset Mgmt., Inc., 694 F. 2d 923, 929 (2d Cir. 1982), to connote the Senate's awareness of "potentially incestuous" behavior.
[121] Birdthistle
[122] Bogle.
[123] "BlackRock's Larry Fink paid nearly $26 million in 2015." http://www.reuters.com/article/us-blackrock-compensation-ceo-idUSKCN0WK2OA. (Accessed February 28, 2017.)
[124] Johnson, II, Edward. "How the owners of Fidelity get richer at everyday investors' expense. http://www.reuters.com/investigates/special-report/usa-fidelity-family/. (Accessed February 28, 2017)
[125] CNN Money Special Report "Big bank execs: What they take home." http://money.cnn.com/news/specials/storysupplement/ceopay/. (Accessed February 28, 2017)
[126] Braham.
[127] Horizon Kinetics. Indexation: Capitalist Toll - Delivery Agent of The Great Bubble. Grant's Interest Rate Observer. October 4, 2016.
[128] Investopedia. "Investing 101: What Is Investing?" http://www.investopedia.com/university/beginner/beginner1.asp. (Accessed February 28, 2017)
[129] Suster, Mark. "Mark Cuban on Why You Need to Study Artificial Intelligence or You'll be a Dinosaur in 3 Years." https://bothsidesofthetable.com/mark-cuban-on-why-you-need-to-study-artificial-intelligence-or-youll-be-a-dinosaur-in-3-years-db3447bea1b4#.sslve6vcd. (Accessed February 28, 2017)
[130] CNBC. "Warren Buffett's advice to LeBron James." http://www.cnbc.com/2015/03/02/warren-buffetts-advice-to-lebron-james.html March 2nd 2015. (Accessed February 28, 2017)
[131] Russell, Richard. "Rich Man, Poor Mine."

http://dowtheoryletters.com/Content_Free/2494.aspx. (Accessed February 28, 2017).

[132] A lender of last resort is an institution, usually a country's central bank, that offers loans to banks or other eligible institutions that are experiencing financial difficulty or are considered highly risky or near collapse.

[133] "Warren Buffett Tells You How to Handle a Market Crash." https://www.fool.com/investing/general/2014/10/11/warren-buffett-tells-you-how-to-handle-a-market-cr.aspx Oct 11, 2014. (Accessed February 28, 2017.)

[134] Graham.

[135] Jeremy Grantham letter to investors

[136] "BlackRock's Fink jolts ETF business with 'blow up' warning." http://www.reuters.com/article/us-funds-etf-fink-analysis-idUSKBN0EB0HI20140531. (Accessed February 28, 2017)

[137] Gandel, Stephen. 2015. Carl Icahn: BlackRock is an extremely dangerous company. http://fortune.com/2015/07/15/carl-icahn-blackrock-is-an-extremely-dangerous-company/

[138] "Carl Icahn: BlackRock is an extremely dangerous company." http://fortune.com/2015/07/15/carl-icahn-blackrock-is-an-extremely-dangerous-company/. (Accessed February 28, 2017)

www.ingramcontent.com/pod-product-compliance
Lightning Source LLC
Chambersburg PA
CBHW061438180526
45170CB00004B/1461